The Henry Root Letters

I WISH to protest most
strongly about everything.
—Henry Root, Park Walk.
West Brompton.

EVENING STANDARD, WEDNESDAY, AUGUST 15, 1979

Henry Root

The Henry Root Letters

Macdonald Futura Publishers

A Futura Book

First published in Great Britain in 1980
by Weidenfeld & Nicolson Ltd

First Futura edition 1981

Copyright © Henry Root 1980

ISBN 0 7088 1888 9

Photoset by
Rowland Phototypesetting Ltd
Bury St Edmunds, Suffolk
Printed on Super Snowbulk 60 gsm
supplied by Holmen Hellefos
Printed in Great Britain by
Hazell, Watson & Viney
Aylesbury, Bucks

Macdonald Futura Publishers Ltd
Paulton House
8 Shepherdess Walk
London N1 7LW

To Mrs Root and Mrs Thatcher: two ordinary mothers

139 Elm Park Mansions
Park Walk
London, S.W.10.

Lord Weidenfeld,
Weidenfeld & Nicolson Ltd,
91 Clapham High Street,
London, S.W.4.   8th June 1979.

Dear Lord Weidenfeld,

I enclose the synopsis of my original novel 'Day of Reckoning', together with correspondence relating to this work between myself and the house of Jonathan Cape Ltd.

Reading between the lines of their letters, you will agree, I think, that they came within a whisker of publishing it. There is certainly little doubt that they found the second draft a great improvement on the first.

What's your honest opinion? I'm addressing myself to you personally as the head of the firm since one of the mistakes I made with Cape, I think, was not to insist that the matter be dealt with by Cape himself.

I like to encourage young people, but not when my own interests are affected. In my experience, it's always best to deal with the big smell at the top. For instance, being a man of the world like myself, you'll appreciate the value of an author who has Nigel Dempsey of 'The Daily Mail' and many of our better literary editors 'in his pocket'.

Is your address all right? I was always led to believe that the Bloomsbury area was where it was all happening publishing-wise. I expect you know what you're doing.

I enclose a stamped addressed envelope for the return of my MS should you think it needs yet further polishing before publication.

I look forward to hearing from you. I've got several other valid ideas for books ready to go!

Yours sincerely,

Henry Root.

Weidenfeld (Publishers) Limited

91 Clapham High Street, London SW4 7TA

Henry Root Esq.,
139 Elm Park Mansions
Park Walk
London SW10   13 June 1979

Dear Mr Root,

Many thanks for your letter of 8 June to Lord
Weidenfeld. I'm glad to say the noble lord is far too busy
making multi-million dollar deals to read anything from
no-hopers, and gets oppressed minions like me to fob
them off as politely as possible.

I would like to congratulate you on your book and make
you an offer you'll find hard to refuse. In return for
£200,000 or a tankful of petrol (whichever is the greater)
we'd be delighted to publish it. I give you a personal
guarantee that under no circumstances would we print
less than six copies or remainder it within two weeks of
publication. You can't be fairer than that, now, can you?

I very much look forward to receiving your cheque by
return of post. I should say that we're currently
reviewing our accounting procedures and for
safekeeping you'd be wise to make it out to *me
personally*.

Yours ever,

Simon Dally

PS Do give my love to Nigs when you're next down at the Daily Mail. Tell him he's a naughty boy to be in both our pockets! You can't serve two masters in my view.

PPS No, our address isn't all right. But I'm looking forward to examining vacant Bloomsbury properties just as soon as I receive your cheque.

139 Elm Park Mansions
Park Walk
London, S.W.10.

Sir David McNee,
New Scotland Yard
London, S.W.1.

21st March 1979.

Dear Sir David,

Hang on! Ignore the media! Ordinary folk are with you all the way in your campaign for greater police powers.

Better that ten innocent men be convicted than that one guilty man goes free! That's what the lounge-room revolutionaries fail to understand.

Don't be depressed by the fact that your 'image' isn't too clever just yet. We have to face it that you come across a wee bit charmless. So what? Do we want this once great country to be policed by the likes of Mr Victor Sassoon the barber and cosmetics expert from Los Angeles?

Your predecessor, Sir Robert Mark, was an accomplished PR man, so it was easy for him. And he had a lot of luck with the 'Spaghetti House Siege Situation'. The public really liked that. What a pity the recent 'Gunman Holed Up In Village Pub Shot Dead By 392 Policeman Situation' didn't happen on your patch! That would have been just the break you needed. As it was, the Chief Constable of Essex was able to pick up the apples on that one. Never mind. Your chance will come.

Here's a pound. Use it to enforce Law and Order.

So – you're doing your poor best, but what can we, the ordinary folk, do? We need you to tell us. The politicians (with the exception of Mrs Thatcher) aren't giving us a lead.

Could you oblige with a photo? I'd like to stick it up in my boy Henry Jr's room in lieu of one of a popular crooning group entitled The Boomtown Rats. The lad's 15, but he's not shaping up. He idles around in his room all day, sewing sequins onto his disco pumps and worse. When I put a photo of Sir Robert Mark on his wall, it was down within seconds and up went the Boomtown crooners again. I'm not usually an advocate of unauthorised violence, but if he takes your picture down I'll knock the wee blighter senseless, that's for sure.

Keep hammering 'em!

Support Mrs Thatcher!

Yours for greater police powers!

Henry Root.

New Scotland Yard

Broadway London SW1H 0BG

29 March 1979

Sir David McNee QPM

Dear Mr Root

The Commissioner has asked me to write and thank you for your letter of 21 March; your kind comments are appreciated.

As requested, I enclose a signed photograph of Sir David. Perhaps I should warn you, however, that the Commissioner keeps a close watch on crime reports and will be keeping a particular eye on them to ensure that you do not do what you propose to do should your son take the photograph off his wall!

I regret that police are not permitted to accept money for the purpose you propose; although the thought is acknowledged I have to return your donation herewith.

Yours sincerely

Brian Gittins
Private Secretary

Mr Henry Root
139 Elm Park Mansions
Park Walk
LONDON SW10

139 Elm Park Mansions
Park Walk
London, S.W.10.

Mrs Margaret Thatcher,
The House of Commons,
London, S.W.1.   23rd March 1979

Dear Leader!

So they said a woman couldn't do it! They were forgetting Joan d'Arc, the maid of Orleans! She put it over the French with their bidets and so-called soixante-neuf and so will you!

Never give up!

This is what we've got to do. With the help of the Scot Nats we can bring down Mr Callaghan and his ramshackle crew of wooly-minded lightweights. At the first suitable opportunity we must table a motion of no confidence in the Government. I'll have to leave this to you. As long as you get your sums right Jim'll be back feeding his pigs and you'll be measuring for new curtains at No 10!

Throughout the coming battle I'll keep you in touch with door-step opinion.

Avarice is patriotic! Here's a pound.

Your man on the door-step,

Henry Root.

PS. Freedom to do as we're told under the law! Let's go!

[13]

139 Elm Park Mansions
Park Walk
London, S.W.10.

Mrs Margaret Thatcher,
The House of Commons,
London, S.W.1.

29th March 1979.

Dear Leader!

Congratulations! You took my advice, you went for the vote of no confidence and now you can start thinking about new colour schemes for No 10!

I believe 'Sunny Jim' is collecting his cards from Her Majesty today. How nice for her to know it's the last she'll be seeing of *him* for a while! She must be looking forward to cosy tea-time chats with another woman such as yourself. Two mothers.

Now, with great respect, a word of advice from an old campaigner. It's been my experience that the weaker sex (God bless 'em!) sometimes hesitate to go for the kill. I'm sure this doesn't apply to you, but now is *not* the time to back off. You've shaken up 'Sunny Jim' with a stiff left hook and now you've got to dump him on his backside with a solid right cross. The old one-two. That's a boxing term. Get your husband, Mr Thatcher, to explain it to you. I read an article about him in 'The Evening Standard' the other day. He sounds like a nice old stick and I think we'd get on well together. The article said he's a simple man who believes in calling a spade a spade. So do I.

Talking about spades, I gather you have one in your Shadow Cabinet – the ex-Gurkha, Mr John Nott. Okay. Fair enough. Nothing wrong with that. Trying to trick in some of the immigrant vote by having one of our Asian friends in your inner circle is a shrewd move on your part. But don't carry the concept too far. Once you've won the election, ditch him.

Another word of advice. In the coming campaign, *don't worry about your voice*. Don't listen to people who say you sound like a suburban estate agent's wife. What's wrong with suburban estate agents? They have a vote!

One last thing. Mrs Root and I have recently formed 'The Ordinary Folk Against Porn Society'. We meet once a week with some of our friends (Dr Littlewinkle and his good lady, the Smithsons, Major Dewdrop and Fred and Rita Snipe, who live opposite, form the hard-core nucleus) to discuss sex, drugs, nudity and violence. While I know these are all subjects that interest you, I expect you'll be too busy at the moment, what with one thing and another, to address us yourself. Don't worry. We understand. However, a signed photograph and message of encouragement would mean a lot to our members.

Don't forget the old one-two!

Your Man on the Door-step!

Henry Root.

House of Commons

London SW1A 0AA.

4th April 1979

Dear Mr Root,

Mrs Thatcher has asked me to thank you for your two recent letters of 23rd and 29th March.

She has asked me to say how grateful she is to you for your kind donation and your very kind words of support. As you request I am sending a photograph of Mrs Thatcher, which she has signed for you.

As far as your request for a message is concerned, I am afraid because of the forthcoming campaign Mrs Thatcher has so many pressures on her time that it is not possible for her to write one personally.

She hopes you will understand the reasons for this reluctant refusal, and asked me to pass on her best wishes.

Yours sincerely,

Richard Ryder
Private Office

Henry Root Esq

139 Elm Park Mansions
Park Walk
London, S.W.10.

The Chairman,
Faber & Faber Ltd,
London, W.C.1.   23rd March 1979.

Dear Sir,

Subject to certain stipulations, I'd be prepared to accept the post of commissioning editor, as advertised in 'The Spectator' this week.

I had my people check you out thoroughly and I have to tell you they ran into a lot of negative feedback. The word on the literary scene is that the once respected name of Faber and Faber isn't too sweet just now.

Never mind. I can stop the rot. Books aren't my business, but that's neither here nor there these days. Basic commercial principles are the same whether you're selling poetry or wet fish (my dodge, as it happens.) Don't get me wrong. I rub along all right with books. In fact I quite like them. The trouble is they don't like me. Still, who reads books? You've got to diversify, up-date the product, smarten up the image – or go to the wall.

Who's selling really BIG now? Writers? Not a chance! The punters are buying Ustinov, Niven, Betty Bacall, Diana Dors, Dr J. P. R. Williams, Sir Robert Mark, Lady Antonia Fraser as was, Ted Heath, Shirley Conran (the cook) and the vet from the Midlands.

Have you the faintest idea how many copies of David Niven's books have sold world-wide to date?

9½ million! That means there's a hell of a lot of mugs out there, and we've got to reach them!

I can show you how. Of course we'll run into a lot of trouble with the grey-beards on your board and I'm afraid they'll have to go. Leave this to me. As I say, my background is business systems and wet fish and I'm happy to be the goon with the big hatchet.

I've a lot of solid contacts abroad – particularly in Iceland, South Africa, Rhodesia, Turkey and Chile – and a stack of valid ideas which could put you back on the literary map.

As luck would have it I'll be in your neck of the woods of Tuesday 3rd April, so unless I hear that it would be inconvenient for you I'll hop through your door at about 12.30.

We can tie up the details (salary, expenses etc) then.

Yours faithfully,

Henry Root.

Faber and Faber Ltd

Publishers

3 Queen Square, London WC1N 3AU

28th March, 1979

Henry Root, Esq.,
139 Elm Park Mansions,
Park Walk,
London, S.W.10.

Dear Mr. Root,

We are grateful to you for having answered our advertisement about the editorial vacancy here. We had a very large number of replies and we have now compiled a short list of those people whom we would like to interview. I very much regret to have to let you know that, after having considered your application very carefully, we have decided not to include your name on this list.

Do please let me say again how grateful we are to you for having written to us.

Yours sincerely,

Henrietta Smith
Secretary to the Chairman

P.S. The Chairman has asked me to add that there would be no point in your calling in here on Tuesday morning, though he is grateful to you for your offer to do so.

Mr James Anderton,
The Chief Constable,
Greater Manchester,
Manchester.   23rd March 1979.

Dear Chief Constable,

Your stand against the porno merchants of
Manchester is an inspiration to ordinary folk down here
in the soft south. Our own Sir David McNee is doing his
poor best, but the odds are against him. He's a fine
man, but the Hampstead pansies have got him by the
tail.

We have to keep asserting that people commit crimes
not because they come from so-called deprived
backgrounds, but because they're *wicked*. The statistics
showing that only .00137% of all crimes of senseless
violence are carried out by stockbrokers living in
Sunningdale prove only that such folk are stockbrokers
because they've got a sense of right and wrong – not
vice versa.

Since it's always been my opinion that the fight
against evil shouldn't be left entirely to intellectuals like
yourself, but that the man in the street should play his
part too, Mrs Root and I recently formed 'The Ordinary
Folk Against The Rising Tide of Filth In Our Society
Situation Society' (TOFATRTOFIOSSS for short). We
meet once a week for a lively, no-holds-barred
discussion over wine and cheese and a guest
intellectual delivers a short paper.

We have extended invites to most of the top turns in

the struggle against filth, many of whom will be familiar to you from joint porn-monitoring talk-ins. I'm referring, of course, to Lord Longford, Mary Kenny, Mrs Whitehouse, Mr Philip Wrack, the Dowager Lady Birdwood, Mr Richard West and Sir Emile Littler (or Prince Littler, as he now is, having inherited the title from his brother.) So far we've drawn a complete blank, alas. It's the old story. Intellectuals are very handy with words; less handy, in my experience, when it comes to a bit of direct action.

I realise that cracking down on the porno merchants in Manchester must take up a lot of your time, but is there any chance that you might read us a paper? We would, of course, pay your travelling expenses from Manchester and back.

Keep hitting 'em where it hurts!

'What Manchester thinks today, Hampstead will think in ten years time!' (Richard West.)

Your pal in the soft south,

Henry Root.

C James Anderton, Q.P.M., F.B.I.M.

Chief Constable

Chief Constable's Office
P O Box 22 (S. West PDO)
Chester House
Boyer Street
Manchester M16 0RE

27th March 1979.

Dear Mr. Root,

Thank you for your very kind letter of support which I was most pleased to receive.

Much as I would like to support you and your friends in your worthwhile cause, I regret it will not be possible for me in the foreseeable future to give any address in London or, indeed, elsewhere. My diary of speaking engagements is practically full until the end of 1980.

Thank you for writing to me.

Yours sincerely,

Chief Constable.

H. Root Esq.,
139 Elm Park Mansions,
Park Walk,
London, S.W.10.

139 Elm Park Mansions
Park Walk
London, S.W.10.

Sir Robert Mark,
c/o William Collins & Sons Ltd,
14 St James's Place,
London, S.W.1.   26th March 1979.

Dear Sir Robert,

It was with a deep sense of shock and outrage that I read in 'The Daily Telegraph' recently that you are now driving a breakdown van for the AA and selling life assurance in the evening.

Surely your book, 'In the Office of Constable', didn't sell *that* badly? *I* thought it was good! It could have done with a few more anecdotes, perhaps, along the lines of the amusing incident early in your career when you had at a fellow in the waterworks and then broke his leg. That's the sort of stuff the public likes. Shows the boys in blue to be human like the rest of us. Perhaps it was an isolated incident. I dare say that sort of excitement is just the glamorous side of a policeman's job.

Anyway, here's a pound. Not much, I'm afraid, but if ordinary folk everywhere donated a pound to public servants on their retirement they wouldn't be reduced in their declining years to patrolling the M4 in a yellow van and selling life-assurance door-to-door.

Yours for a better deal for our distressed old folk!

Henry Root.

[23]

139 Elm Park Mansions
Park Walk
London, S.W.10.

The Rt Hon William Whitelaw,
The House of Commons,
London, S.W.1.   28th March 1979.

Dear Mr Whitelaw,

As an ordinary father, I have been much disturbed by two recent remarks by men in public life.

First, in an interview in 'The Evening News', Sir Robert Mark said that he would not be against the decriminalisation of cannabis as long as he could be convinced that the substance had no harmful effects!

Secondly, ex-Chief Superintendent so-called 'Nipper' Reed said in the course of a TV interview with Mr Ludovic Kennedy that when he was a serving officer it had been impossible to investigate serious crimes from Scotland Yard due to the fact that more criminals ran their affairs from there than did upholders of law and order! To catch the so-called Krays he had been compelled to do all his phoning from a kiosk on the corner!

With regard to Sir Robert's amazing observation, small wonder this once great country continues to career down-hill like a greased pig if ex-public servants can openly advocate the decriminalisation of a pleasure for no better reason than that it's harmless!

And the alarming significance of Mr Reed's remark seems to have gone unnoticed. Is it not on all fours with saying that the last place at which one can safely mail a letter is the Post Office?

Can you give me your assurance, Sir, as our future Home Secretary, that cannabis will not be legalised *however harmless it turns out to be* and that under your firm stewardship the police will once again have as much time to investigate crime as they now have to investigate each other?

Support Mrs Thatcher!

Yours Against the Decriminalisation of Harmless Pleasures!

Henry Root.

From: The Rt. Hon. William Whitelaw, C.H., M.C., M.P.

House of Commons

London SW1   0AA

2nd April, 1979

Dear Mr. Root,

Thank you for your letter of 28th March and your very
kind good wishes to our Party and to Margaret
Thatcher.

There is no question of any future Conservative
Government legalising cannabis. We also intend to
build up the strength and the quality of the Police to
give them a better opportunity to investigate and
prevent crime.

Yours sincerely,

William Whitelaw.

H. Root, Esq.,
139 Elm Park Mansions,
Park Walk,
London, S.W.10.

139 Elm Park Mansions
Park Walk
London S.W.10

Ms Esther Rantzen,
BBC Television,
London, W.12.
26th March 1979.

Dear Esther,

Congratulations on another great show last night! The main 'How to get your knickers off' item was hilarious! Both Mrs Root and I chuckled all the way through it.

You've got the formula just right. If only more people in TV (television) realised that it's possible to be healthily vulgar without descending to schoolboy smut.

I enclose some humorous definitions and a comic poem for Cyril. I hope you can use them. On the assumption that you can, I'm invoicing the BBC separately.

Humorous Definitions.

Falsies: An enhancer to a maiden's pair!
The Vatican: House of pill refute!
The three ages of man: Tri-weekly, try weekly and try weakly!
Graffiti in Gents' W.C.: Squatters' writes!

Comical Poem.

While Titian was mixing rose-madder,
His model posed nude on a ladder.
Her position to Titian

Suggested coition,
So he climbed up the ladder and had 'er!

Just one slight criticism of the show last night. I thought your dress was rather revealing for what is essentially family viewing. One could see your legs quite clearly. I hope you won't mind my saying this. One doesn't want to see women's legs in one's lounge-room at a time when youngsters are still up and about.
Could you possibly oblige with a photo?

Yours for A Comical Definition!

Henry Root.

Henry Root,
139 Elm Park Mansions
Park Walk,
London, S.W.10.

The Accounts Department
The BBC
Broadcasting House
Portland Place
London, W.1.   26th March 1979.

INVOICE

To four humorous definitions and one comical poem
for THAT'S LIFE ....£12.95.

Kindly remit and oblige.

British Broadcasting Corporation

Kensington House Richmond Way London W14 0AX

22nd April 1979.

Dear Mr. Root,

Thank you very much indeed for taking the trouble to write to me. Hearing from viewers like yourself is a tremendous morale boost for us all – it really makes a great difference to me to know that you find our work enjoyable and worthwhile. May I send you my best wishes, and thank you again for your letter.

Yours sincerely,

Esther Rantzen

139 Elm Park Mansions
Park Walk
London, S.W.10.

The Accounts Department
The BBC
Broadcasting House
Portland Place
London, W.1.   9th April 1979.

Dear Sir,

On 26th March I sent you an invoice for £12.95 for
some humorous definitions and a comical poem I
submitted to 'That's Life'.

I have not received the money and I must tell you that
unless I get satisfaction by return of post I will be
compelled to put the matter in the hands of my solicitor.

Yours faithfully,

Henry Root.

British Broadcasting Corporation

Kensington House Richmond Way London W14 0AX

Mr H Root
139 Elm Park Mansions
Park Walk
London SW10   22nd April 1979

Dear Mr Root

Your letter of the 9th April 1979 has been forwarded to
me by the BBC Accounts Department.

The That's Life programme does not pay fees for
uncommissioned material that is not transmitted.

Yours sincerely

Henry Murray
Producer, That's Life

139 Elm Park Mansions
Park Walk
London, S.W.10.

Ms Esther Rantzen,
'That's Life',
Television Centre,
London, W.12.   23rd April 1979.

Dear Esther,

You're a fat idiot and your show's a disgrace.

Yours sincerely,

Henry Root.

British Broadcasting Corporation

Kensington House Richmond Way London W14 0AX

26th April 1979

Dear Mr. Root,

Thank you very much indeed for taking the trouble to
write to me. Hearing from viewers like yourself is a
tremendous morale boost for us all – it really makes a
great difference to me to know that you find our work
enjoyable and worthwhile. May I send you my best
wishes, and thank you again for your letter.

Yours sincerely,

Esther Rantzen

139 Elm Park Mansions
Park Walk
London, S.W.10.

Ray Cooney Esq,
The Whitehall Theatre,
London, S.W.1.

29th March 1979.

Dear Cooney,

Mrs Root and I saw your show 'Ipi Tombi' last night.
Better late than never! We both thoroughly enjoyed it
and the nudity, being ethnic, was for once entirely
inoffensive. I hope you won't mind my saying this. I
assume from your name that you yourself are one of our
coloured friends. Nothing wrong with that. Good luck
to you!

Anyway, it struck me that a hit show must make quite
a handy profit. Do you look for outside investors –
fairies, I think you call them?

The fact is I've been in fish all my life, I've worked
hard, saved hard and now I reckon I could afford a small
flutter without breaking the bank. I'm talking about just
a few thousand, spread over several shows to minimise
the risk. I believe the accident rate is quite high in your
business.

I hope you won't mind my asking. I'd really
appreciate the opportunity to invest if it's at all possible,
and I'd like to encourage someone from your part of the
world.

I look forward to hearing from you.

Yours sincerely,

Henry Root.

[34]

139 Elm Park Mansions
Park Walk
London, S.W.10.

Michael Edwardes Esq,
British Leyland Ltd,
Marylebone Road,
London, N.W.1.   31st March 1979.

Dear Mr Edwardes,

As a patriot, I am becoming increasingly distressed by the fact that the mere mention of 'British Leyland' by a music-hall comedian gives rise to gales of ignorant laughter, rather as the conjoined notions of Her Royal Highness Princess Anne and a horse are liable to take the roof off the London Palladium if mentioned from the stage in the course of one of Lord Delfont's Royal Variety Shows.

I would remind you, Sir, that every time someone laughs at 'British Leyland' they are laughing at Great Britain.

In the circumstances I would earnestly suggest that you change the name of the company either to 'Japanese Leyland' or to 'Jamaican Leyland'.

The only jokes ever made about the Japanese concentrate round the fact that they tend to be extremely small (like yourself – nothing wrong with that) and that they are clever little monkeys who work too hard.

Jokes along these lines would only be good for your company's image. And if jokes were made about 'Jamaican Leyland' you could prosecute the offenders under the Race Discrimination Act.

I look forward to hearing your reaction to this suggestion.

Yours sincerely,

Henry Root. Patriot!

139 Elm Park Mansions
Park Walk
London, S.W.10.

D. Dudley Morgan Esq,
Theodore Goddard & Co,
16 St Martin-le-Grand,
London, E.C.1.   7th April 1979.

Dear Mr Morgan,

   Your firm has been recommended to me as being one
with some experience of the law. I address myself to
you personally as the senior partner since I have
litigation of some import to prosecute and I don't wish
to find myself in the hands of the office-boy.

   As the enclosed documents will show, I wrote to Mr
Michael Edwardes of British Leyland on the 31st March
with the viable suggestion that the name of the
company be changed to 'Japanese Leyland'.

   As you will imagine, it was with a sense of outrage
that I discovered on 4th April that my concept was
already in the pipeline. By 5th April the matter had
become public knowledge, as the enclosed cartoon will
adequately demonstrate.

   Mr Edwardes has not favoured me with the courtesy
of a reply to my letter and I am now persuaded that he is
of a mind to 'borrow' my notion without
acknowledgement or payment.

   You will agree that in the circumstances damages of
unusual consequence would come my way in the High
Court.

   I look forward to hearing that you will act for me in

this matter. I am in a position to put further work your way pursuant to a satisfactory assessment of your performance hereunder.

Yours faithfully,

Henry Root.

Theodore Goddard & Co.

16 St. Martin's-Le-Grand
London EC1A 4EJ

H. Root, Esq.,
139 Elm Park Mansions,
Park Walk,
London, S.W.10.   12th April, 1979.

Dear Sir,

Thank you for your letter of 7th April with enclosures concerning your possible complaint against Mr. Michael Edwards of British Leyland. I do not think I would necessarily agree with the penultimate paragraph of your letter that in the circumstances considerable damages would be awarded to you in the High Court.

In the circumstances this would not be a case which this firm would be prepared to undertake, and had we been prepared to do so we would have required very substantial sums on account before we accepted any instructions. If you still wish to proceed I suggest you seek some other firm who will be prepared to accept your instructions.

Yours faithfully,

D. DUDLEY MORGAN

139 Elm Park Mansions
Park Walk
London, S.W.10.

Eric Levine Esq,
Eric Levine & Co,
63 Lincoln's Inn Fields,
London, W.C.2.   17th April 1979.

Dear Mr Levine,

I would like to instruct you in two pertinent matters.

As the enclosed letter will show, I wrote to Mr
Michael Edwardes of British Leyland on 31st March
suggesting that the name of the company be changed to
'Japanese Leyland'. It was with a deep sense of outrage
that I discovered through 'the media' on 4th April that
my concept had been taken up and acted on. By 5th
April the matter had become public knowledge and a
source of humour in popular papers.

Mr Edwardes has not favoured me with the courtesy
of a reply to my various letters of protest (indeed he
appears to have gone to ground – as well he might!)
and it now seems certain that he intends to appropriate
my idea without payment.

I think you will agree that in the circumstances
punitive damages would be awarded to me in the High
Court.

The other matter is somewhat more trivial. As the
enclosed documents will show, I recently submitted
four comical definitions and a humorous poem to
Esther Rantzen's excellent TV Show 'That's Life'. I have
chased up the BBC's accounts department, but so far no

money has been forthcoming and I judge that now is the time to sue them.

I look forward to hearing that you can act for me with your customary vigour in these two matters.

Yours sincerely,

Henry Root.

Eric Levine & Co.

63 Lincoln's Inn Fields London WC2A 3LW

H. Root, Esq.,
139 Elm Park Mansions,
Park Walk,
London SW 10   24th April 1979

Dear Mr. Root,

I thank you for your letter of 17th April addressed to
Mr. Levine.

Mr. Levine is presently abroad and will be travelling
significantly over the next several weeks. I will of course
pass your letter to him when he is next in London. It
may be that you would wish to pass your letters to
somebody who will have a greater amount of time
available to deal with the matter.

Yours sincerely,

KAY TALBOT
Secretary to:
ERIC LEVINE

139 Elm Park Mansions
Park Walk
London, S.W.10.

Ms Kay Talbot,
Eric Levine & Co,
63 Lincoln's Inn Fields,
London, W.C.2.   26th April 1979.

Dear Ms Talbot,

Thank you for your letter of 24th April with regard to the matter between British Leyland and myself.

I'm sorry to hear that Mr Levine is abroad and travelling 'significantly' over the next several weeks. Nothing amiss, I hope?

I'm particularly eager to prosecute this bit of litigation with all due haste and since I have heard such excellent things about your firm I am wondering whether one of the other partners might handle the dodge for me?

I see the name of Mr Keith Fletcher at the top of your writing paper. Would this by any chance be the Keith Fletcher (known affectionately to his team-mates as 'The Gnome') who skippers Essex at cricket? If so, I would be more than happy for him to handle the caper for me. He's a wily skipper who reads the game well and although I've seen him drop a couple of sitters in the slips in my time, I'm sure he won't be a butter-fingers with this one!

It so happens that I'll be in your part of the world next Friday 4th May, so unless I hear that it would be inconvenient I'll drop by at 12.30 for an initial conference with 'The Gnome'.

Yours sincerely,

Henry Root.

Eric Levine & Co.

63 Lincoln's Inn Fields, London WC2A 3LW

H. Root, Esq.,
139 Elm Park Mansions,
Park Walk,
London SW 10   27th April 1979

Dear Mr. Root,

I thank you for your letter of 26th April the content of which together with your earlier letter I have now had the opportunity of discussing with Mr. Levine.

Mr. Levine regrets that he is not able to act for you in this matter since it is not the type of matter that the firm deals with.

Yours sincerely,

KAY TALBOT
Secretary to:
ERIC LEVINE

139 Elm Park Mansions
Park Walk
London, S.W.10.

Mr 'Larry' Lamb,
The Sun,
30 Bouverie Street,
London, E.C.4.

31st March 1979.

Dear Mr Lamb,

As a 'Sun' reader for many years (Mrs Root chaffs me
that I only take it for the pretty girls – but what's wrong
with a pretty girl!!?), may I say how shocked I was this
morning to read the following story on your TV page?

'Fun-loving Ian McShane could not resist the
temptation to send-up the Last Supper while 'Jesus of
Nazareth' was being filmed. McShane, 36, who plays
Judas, says: "I had to sneak out of the door with evil in
my heart, to betray Christ. I sneaked out all right –
then I stuck my head back round the door and said: 'I
have got it right, haven't I? Five hake, two rock salmon,
five plaice and twelve chips?' They all fell about!" It was
just one of the many zany things that happened during
the making of 'Jesus of Nazareth' (ITV, Sunday 6.30) in
Morocco . . .'

It's one thing for some prancing mime to act the goat
at a poignant moment in Our Lord's story; quite
another for a family newspaper such as yours to report
his oafish antics with apparent approval.

Don't misunderstand me. I'm no 'Disgusting of
Tunbridge Wells'. I've knocked around the world and
so has Mrs Root. We like a bit of harmless fun as much
as the next couple (Fred and Rita Snipe in 138). Nudity
(and yours is always tasteful) is all right in its place;
blasphemy, on the other hand, is below the belt.

[45]

I look forward to receiving your explanation for this deplorable lapse and to your confirmation that the journalist responsible, Chris Kenworthy, has been relieved of his position.

Yours sincerely,

Henry Root.

Copies to:
The Press Council.
Lord Grade.
Mrs Whitehouse.
Lord Goodman.
Mary Kenny.

139 Elm Park Mansions
Park Walk
London, S.W.10.

Lord Grade,
ATV,
17 Great Cumberland Place,
London, W.1.   31st March 1979.

Dear Lord Grade,

Since I have always assumed that you are a religious man in the widest sense of the word (albeit of a different faith to that of myself, Mrs Root and Mary Kenny) as well as being a man with an eye for a profit (and what's wrong with that?), I thought you would be interested in the enclosed letter which I have sent this morning to Mr 'Larry' Lamb, Editor-in-Chief of Sun Newspapers.

I assume that you would not wish your fine and always tasteful TV film 'Jesus of Nazareth' to be the occasion of cheap jokes by unthinking actors.

Yours sincerely,

Henry Root.

P.S. When are we to have the pleasure of Miss Shirley McLaine on our screens again? Now there's a *thinking* actress, who appeals to the whole family.

THE SUN

30 Bouverie Street, Fleet Street, London EC4Y 8DE

Henry Root, Esq.,
139, Elm Park Mansions,
Park Walk,
London, SW10.   April 3rd, 1979.

Dear Mr Root,

Thank you for your letter.

I am sorry you were offended by the McShane story. It is never any part of our purpose to offend.

I agree, on reflection, that the story may well strike some people as being in dubious taste. But we didn't invent it, nor did we necessarily approve. We just reported.

And I really don't think I can sack Mr. Kenworthy for what was, at worst, a relatively minor misjudgment.

Now that *would* be below the belt!

With best wishes,

Yours sincerely,

Larry Lamb
EDITOR.

Associated Communications Corporation Limited

11th April, 1979.

Dear Mr. Root,

Thank you for your note of March 31st with the attached correspondence.

I know that all the actors in our "JESUS OF NAZARETH" production worked extremely hard over a long period and many of them said afterwards, how being involved in the production helped to renew their faith in their particular religious beliefs. Young actors working in difficult circumstances may be forgiven moments of high spirits and I feel the newspapers may have exaggerated this out of all proportion.

I am sorry if you found the particular incident disturbing, but knowing Ian McShane, I am confident that this has been related out of context.

Yours sincerely,

(Lord Grade)

Mr. Henry Root

Her Majesty the Queen (and Duke of Normandy!)
Buckingham Palace,
London, S.W.1.   9th April 1979.

Your Majesty,

With the greatest respect, I take leave to surmise that
as a mother you will be no less concerned than Mrs Root
is about this once great nation's collapse in terms of
moral leadership.

I appreciate that under the constitution you cannot
poke your nose into things too directly, but I do have a
small suggestion to make.

You're always opening things: hospitals, schools,
theatres, factories, fly-overs, play-grounds etc.

Why don't you *close* a few things?

I have in mind such blemishes on the face of our
society as The National Liberal Club, BBC 2, Soho's
'foreign' cinemas and so-called massage parlours, the
National Council for Civil Liberties, subversive
periodicals such as 'The New Statesman' and 'Time
Out', which are devoted to the undermining of family
life and our British institutions, and the new white tile
universities, which see it as their function to stuff the
impressionable young students with half-baked left-
wing notions.

With great respect, Ma'am, I shouldn't have to
remind you how gratified your late grandmother,

Queen Victoria, would have been to see you give the nation a moral lead in these matters.

Support Mrs Thatcher!

Royalists demand the return of the rope!

Your humble subject,

Henry Root.

BUCKINGHAM PALACE.

The Private Secretary is

commanded by Her Majesty The Queen

to thank Mr. H. Root

for his letter of 9th April.

12th April. 1979

139 Elm Park Mansions
Park Walk
London, S.W.10.

Miss Angela Rippon,
BBC News,
Television Centre,
London, W.12.   9th April 1979.

Dear Miss Rippon,

I and many millions of your admirers must have been disappointed to read in the paper yesterday that you plan to sue the Mirror Group for calling you the 'Iron Maiden'.

What is insulting or damaging about such a cognomen? Is not our future Leader, Mrs Thatcher, known as 'The Iron Lady'? What could be a greater honour than to be associated in the public consciousness with such a fine woman?

I gather that you think the name suggests that you are some sort of lemon-faced puritan. What's wrong with that? Surely a liberated woman such as yourself doesn't want to be thought of as a scatter-brained sex-symbol, subjected each night to the insulting stares of frustrated men who think women are for one thing only? Your admirers like you just the way you are.

Could you possibly send me a photograph of Anna Ford? I'd write to her myself, but as I'm already writing to you it seems silly to waste a stamp.

Yours sincerely,

Henry Root.

P.S. In case you intend to pursue your mistaken action for damages, I enclose a pound to help with the costs. I don't approve of what you are doing, but I'd like to support you all the same. I also enclose the postage for Anna Ford's photograph. Thank you.

British Broadcasting Corporation

Television Centre, Wood Lane London W12 7RJ

Dear Mr Root,

What an extraordinary letter!

I *have* sued the Mirror Group – *not* for calling me an "Iron maiden" but for a 2 page article in Revallie which contained *numerous* accusations and slanderous comments.

You are obviously a man of intelligence – why then such a conclusion from a paraphrased note when you would have been able to make an informed observation (and an accurate one) by reading the full article.

As I have won the case I have no costs, so I return your contribution with thanks.

Yours sincerely,

Angela Rippon

139 Elm Park Mansions
Park Walk
London, S.W.10.

The Lucie Clayton Model Agency,
168 Brompton Road,
London, S.W.1.   9th April 1979.

Dear Sir or Madame,

Once a year the officers and men of the Rifle Brigade meet to discuss old times in the course of a knees-up. Yours truly is the Organising Secretary of this year's get-together which is to be held in a private suite at the Savoy Hotel on Friday 25th May.

I'd like you to supply the cabaret. What we have in mind are a dozen or so 'models' to jump out of a cake and 'mingle' with the guests.

I naturally don't want to be too explicit in a letter, but perhaps I should emphasise that the 'models' should be top types and would be expected to 'go a bit', if you follow me.

We would be prepared to pay each girl a minumum of £100 for the evening's work, and no girl would be required to 'go with' more than six officers or two men.

I look forward to doing business with you.

Yours sincerely,

Henry Root.

Lucie Clayton

168 Brompton Road London SW3 1HW

Henry Root Esq
139 Elm Park Mansions
London SW10

4th May 1979

Dear Mr Root

Neither the Savoy Hotel, nor the adjutant of your
former regiment, confirm your statement about the
25th May and certainly you are writing to the wrong
agency. I have, however, been on to the Provost-
Marshal's department who will be sending some men
to see what it is that you really need.

Yours sincerely

S Neill
REGISTRAR

139 Elm Park Mansions
Park Walk
London, S.W.10.

The Registrar,
Lucie Clayton Ltd,
168 Brompton Road,
London, S.W.3.

5th May 1979.

Dear Miss Neill,

I don't understand. It was the Provost Marshal who recommended you in the first place.

Yours sincerely,

Henry Root.

139 Elm Park Mansions
Park Walk
London, S.W.10.

Miss Mary Kenny,
The Sunday Telegraph,
Fleet Street,
London, E.C.4.   12th April 1979.

Dear Miss Kenny,

May I say how much I appreciate your articles in 'The
Sunday Telegraph' with their emphasis on the need at
this time to affirm the importance of family life?

They are an inspiration in these days of sexual
pleasure off the leash.

I wonder if I could ask your advice on a matter of
dispute between Mrs Root and myself? I hold that oral
contraception is only necessary if you indulge in oral
sex, but Mrs Root argues otherwise.

I would stress that this has nothing to do with the
personal life of myself and Mrs Root. I did my duty by
her many years ago – we have two grand youngsters.
Doreen (19) and Henry Jr (15) – and of course oral sex
never came into it in those days. No, the matter has
arisen because Doreen plans to go on holiday this
summer with a male student from Essex University.
Mrs Root thinks she should have a word in her ear
about 'precautions', however unpleasant this may be
for both of them.

I write to you because you seem like a valid, caring
person. I expect you get literally millions of letters a
week from confused ordinary folk, so I enclose the

return postage to facilitate the convenience of your advice.

I read somewhere that you're writing a book about the meaning of God. That's one to look forward to! Well done!

Yours for the Family!

Henry Root.

139 Elm Park Mansions
Park Walk
London, S.W.10.

The London Theatre Organiser,
British Actors Equity,
8 Harley Street,
London, W.1.   17th April 1979.

Dear Sir or Madam,

This is to inform you that Root Touring Productions Ltd will be holding open auditions for its next attraction – 'The English Way of Doing Things' by Henry Root – on the evening of Tuesday 24th April, at 9.30 at the above address.

Artistes will be required to disrobe frontally and show themselves available in all positions to undertake acts of simulated intercourse for the benefit of myself (choreographer) and Mr and Mrs Snipe (investors) who live next-door.

It is my understanding that an Official Equity Observer likes to be present at such times, and who shall blame him? Nice work if you can get it!

I look forward to meeting your representative on 24th April at 9.30.

Yours for Family Entertainment!

Henry Root.

```
T
 889077 PO FD G
 299992 PO TS G


J172 1734 LONDON T SW 18


HENRY ROOT 139 ELM PARK MANSIONS PARK WALK
LONDONSW10


CONTACT EQUITY URGENT .
      MIKE CHATTIN OR CATHY ALLEN


139 10 .



 889077 PO FD G
 299992 PO TS G
```

139 Elm Park Mansions
Park Walk
London, S.W.10.

Sir Aubrey Melford Stevenson,
Truncheons,
Winchelsea,
East Sussex.   16th April 1979.

M'Lud,

So – this is a sad day for Law and Order! A sad day
too for the ordinary man in the street who asks nothing
more of life than that his women-folk should be able to
go about their business without having first to be rigged
out with an 'Anti-Rape System' or 'Personal Protection
Kit' now being marketted by the excellent firm of
Personal Hazard Protection Ltd, of 69 Silvertown Way,
London E.16 (Tel No 01-476-5648, should you want to
give them a ring.)

Equally, it's a day of celebration for softies, sapphists,
kid-glove pansies, liberals and sodomites.

Here's a pound. Not much, I'm afraid, but if ordinary
folk everywhere gave a pound to great public servants
on their retirement they wouldn't be reduced, like that
fine man Sir Robert Mark, to driving breakdown vans
for the AA, selling life assurance door-to-door, working
as masseurs in so-called 'health farms' and, most
humiliating of all, perhaps, appearing in deodorant ads
on TV.

God bless you, M'Lud!

Yours for Law and Order!

Henry Root.

Truncheons
Winchelsea
Sussex

18 April 1979

Dear Mr Root,

Thank you so much for your letter and all the kind
things you say. I much appreciate them.

As to the pound you so generously sent I have
thought it right to hand it over to the Sussex Police
Welfare fund which I know does valuable work in
helping gallant Police and their families when they
need it. I am sure you will agree with this course as I am
precluded from receiving personal gifts.

I enclose the receipt. You may get a further
acknowledgement from their Headquarters.

Yours v. sincerely

Melford Stevenson

139 Elm Park Mansions
Park Walk
London, S.W.10.

Mr Richard Ryder,
Conservative Party H.Q.,
32 Smith Square,
London, S.W.1.   17th April 1979.

Dear Ryder,

Sorry I haven't been in touch since 29th March! I've been up to my eyebrows in it. I expect you have too. I'm now catching up with my correspondence and am resolved not to fall so badly behind again. Please convey my apologies to Mrs Thatcher.

I am addressing myself to you and have marked this letter 'Private and Confidential' since I want to touch on a rather delicate matter concerning our Leader's health and one which I judge to be best discussed between men. (No doubt Mrs Thatcher, in her courageous way, would deny that anything was wrong.)

The fact is I read in my paper the other day that a Dr Patrick Cosgrave is a constant and close attendant on her. Wishing to discover the precise nature of her complaint, I took advantage of a consultation with my own doctor (don't worry! – just my annual blood pressure read-out) to persuade him to check out Dr Cosgrave's speciality in the BMA register of practitioners.

Imagine our sense of mystification when we found *no one* of this name qualified to practise medicine in the British Isles!

Eventually my doctor surmised that Dr Cosgrave must be a chiropodist, explaining that practitioners of this trade often attach the prefix 'Dr' to their names, though not officially encouraged to do so.

Does our Leader suffer from corns? These can be the very devil, as Mrs Root would be the first to tell you. With so many electoral walk-abouts to do, it seems to be a tantamount priority that Mrs Thatcher should rest up as much as possible and eschew tight shoes.

Mrs Root was once bed-ridden for three weeks. No great hardship for the country in her case, but the people can ill-afford Mrs Thatcher's absence from the centre of things for a like period.

Here's a pound. Persuade our Leader to take it easy. I'll leave this to you.

Bring back the rope!

Yours sincerely,

Henry Root.

From

The Rt. Hon. Mrs Margaret Thatcher

Conservative & Unionist Central Office, 32 Smith Square,
Westminster SW1P 3HH

18th April 1979

Dear Mr Root,

Thank you very much for your letter of 17th April.

Dr Cosgrave has, I believe, a PhD. This is as you know an academic qualification not a medical one. Dr Cosgrave has never claimed to be a doctor of medicine.

Finally thank you for your very kind contribution. It is greatly appreciated.

With best wishes,

Richard Ryder
Private Office

H Root Esq

139 Elm Park Mansions
Park Walk
London, S.W.10.

Dr Dawid de Villiers,
The South African Embassy,
South Africa House,
London, W.C.2.   17th April 1979.

Your Excellency!

May I say what a rare pleasure it is to have a running scrum-half at the Court of St James? I don't usually agree with dragging sport into politics, but I'm happy to make an exception in your case.

I saw you play a few times in your youth, Sir, and by jingo you could go a bit! I know what goes on in those scrummages unperceived by the naked eye in the stands and I never saw you elbow an opponent in the eye or squeeze a fellow's under-parts. You were a gentlemen scrum-half, Sir.

Because of the internal difficulties of your great country (which Mrs Root and I had the great pleasure of visiting a year or two ago) you'll run into a bit of flack over here from ignorant elements in our society: professional liberals who, at a safe distance, like to protest at the robust methods by which your hard-pressed security police uphold the law. I don't have to tell you not to pay any attention. Peter so-called Hain has no constituency. What does he know of your country's internal difficulties? It's an intolerable impertinence, in my opinion, for the citizens of one country to criticise the customs of another, and I hope very much that, in the course of your stay with us, you'll be outspoken in your own criticisms of anyone in this country who holds an opposing view.

Could you oblige with a photograph? As a philosopher and a diplomat you may disapprove of personality cults, but I'm trying to persuade my boy Henry Jr (15) that soccer's a girl's game and I reckon that a photo of a fine looking man like you in his room might do the trick.

Up the Springboks!

We haven't forgotten Rorke's Drift even if the Zulus have!

Yours Against Interfering in the Internal Affairs of Another Country!

Henry Root.

South African Embassy

London WC2N 5DP

Mr Henry Root
139 Elm Park Mansions
Park Walk
London SW 10   25 April 1979

Dear Mr Root

Thank you very much for your friendly letter and warm
words of welcome. Your very kind remarks about me
are sincerely appreciated.

I am delighted to hear that you have visited South
Africa and have gained a favourable impression of our
country. We do not ignore the fact that we have
pressing problems. However these problems are much
more complicated than what most critics are prepared
to acknowledge. I am convinced that the peoples of
South Africa are in the best position to solve their own
problems and will do so, given the opportunity. The
majority of the people in South Africa, black and white,
are dedicated to resolve the problems in a peaceful and
evolutionary way. Great strides have already been
taken in that direction.

It gives me pleasure to oblige you in your request for a
photo for Henry.

Yours sincerely

Dr D J de Villiers
Ambassador

139 Elm Park Mansions
Park Walk
London, S.W.10.

Nicholas Scott MP,
Chelsea Conservative Party,
1a Chelsea Manor Street,
London, S.W.1.   17th April 1979.

Dear Mr Scott,

Don't get me wrong – I'm a Tory, always have been, always will be. However, before casting my vote for you in the coming election I would like to be reassured on one point.

Are you, like our Leader Mrs Thatcher, committed to the re-introduction of selective hanging? If you are, I'm afraid I will be unable, as a matter of conscience, to vote for you.

The concept's nonsense, and the one plank in her platform on which I and Mrs Thatcher (with whom I have been in close touch throughout the campaign) are unable to agree.

Was the Battle of Britain won by shooting down Jerry selectively? I should say not! We pranged the buggers willy-nilly! Now that we are engaged in another, and no less desperate, Battle of Britain we can be certain of one thing: we won't defeat the enemy in our midst – terrorists, weirdos and extremists under the bed – by hanging them selectively. We've got to hang the lot!

I look forward to hearing that you agree with me on this vital issue.

Here's a pound.

Yours for Law and Order!

Henry Root.

Nicholas Scott Conservative

**General Election
3rd May 1979**

Chelsea
Campaign Headquarters
1a Chelsea Manor Street,
London, S.W.3.

20 April 1979

Dear Mr Root

Thank you very much indeed for your contribution to
the Fighting Fund. Like you, I do not approve of
selective hanging!

Yours sincerely

Nicholas Scott

Henry Root Esq,
139 Elm Park Mansions
Park Walk, London, S.W.10.

139 Elm Park Mansions
Park Walk
London, S.W.10.

Nicholas Scott MP,
1a Chelsea Manor Street,
London, S.W.3.   26th April 1979.

Dear Mr Scott,

Thank you for your letter of 20th April, but you will forgive me if I say your answer to my question on selective hanging was somewhat evasive (typical of a politician!)

'Like you, I do not approve of selective hanging', you write. You will agree that this is rather ambiguous to say the least. It might mean that you are against *all* hanging (though I can scarcely bring myself to believe this of a Tory) or it might mean that, like me, you think everyone should be hanged.

It's not in my nature to be a bore, and I must apologise for being so persistent on this point. It's most important to me, however to get an unambiguous reply before voting for you on 3rd May.

Here's another pound!

Up our Leader!

Yours Against Bennery Under the Bed,

Henry Root.

P.S. Talking about beds, may I say – without straying into impertinence, I hope – that I trust all is now well between you and Mrs Scott? It's always sad when the private lives of our public servants are at sixes and sevens, and it must be said that Tories tend to be rather weak-willed and easily-led in these matters.

Nicholas Scott Conservative

**General Election
3rd May 1979**

Chelsea
Campaign Headquarters
1a Chelsea Manor Street,
London, S.W.3.

26 April 1979

Dear Mr Root

Thank you for your further contribution.

I am sorry you found my reaction ambiguous but I really did think my views on this matter were well known in the constituency.

I share the views of those of my colleagues in the Tory Party who are opposed to the principle of capital punishment. This is not to say I am against convicted terrorists spending the rest of their natural lives in gaol, but I do not accept that the threat of hanging is a deterrent to murder and indeed as far as terrorists are concerned my fear is that it could be tragically counter-productive.

Thank you for the kind thoughts behind your personal enquiry. I do not want to be evasive, but just at this special moment in time I can only reassure you that all is well.

Yours sincerely,

Nicholas Scott.

Henry Root Esq.

Richard Ryder Esq,
Conservative Central Office,
32 Smith Square,
London, S.W.1.   26th April 1979.

Dear Ryder,

Many thanks for your letter of 18th April.

It was a great relief to discover that Dr Cosgrave is not, after all, a chiropodist and indeed that our Leader is in perfect health.

May I say how delighted I was to read in yesterday's 'Evening Standard' that our Leader doesn't 'wish to see the death penalty used a very great deal'. This dispels the popular idea that she intends to be personally present at all hangings. This seems to be to be the right attitude. She should only attend the more important ones.

May I also take this opportunity of saying how pleased I was to read in 'The Sun' today that she has written personally to Mrs Whitehouse, giving that good lady her personal guarantee that she will crack down hard on the porno merchants when she comes to power. I see that young Mr Steel characteristically failed to join in the dialogue with Mrs Whitehouse on this vital topic. The boy has no feel for the relevant issues. Mrs Thatcher understands that our leaders ignore Mrs Whitehouse at their peril. She doesn't have to be reminded of what happened to those easily-led light-weights, me noble Lords Lambton and Jellicoe. (You'll notice that I deliberately failed to mention Mr Profumo.

It's high time, in my opinion, that the poor man should be allowed to forget that he slept with a tart, endangered the security of his country and lied to the House of Commons.)

Here's a pound. Use it to crack down on the porno barons.

Bring back the rope!

Your Man on the Door-Step!

Henry Root.

P.S. Henry Root's no tell-tale but I think you ought to know that I've had a most unsatisfactory letter from Nicholas Scott (my local MP) on the subject of selective hanging. Is it too late to put up another candidate in this area?

Copy to Nicholas Scott MP.

From

The Rt. Hon. Mrs Margaret Thatcher

Conservative & Unionist Central Office, 32 Smith Square,
Westminster SW1P 3HH

1st May 1979

Dear Mr Root,

Thank you very much for your kind letter of 26th April.
I am most grateful to you for sending £1 towards our
Campaign Fund. It is much appreciated.

With best wishes.

Richard Ryder
Private Office

Henry Root Esq

139 Elm Park Mansions
Park Walk
London, S.W.10.

Duke Hussey,
The Times,
New Printing House Square,
Gray's Inn Road,
London, W.C.1.   18th April 1979.

Your Grace,

I want you to know that Mrs Root and I were inspired by your performance on 'The News' last night.

Never go down to the Unions! That's not the way to beat the extremists under the bed.

"We plan to change the philosophy of Fleet Street," you said.

Well, I don't know much about philosophy (I left school at sixteen) but I do know I didn't get to the top in fish by truckling to militants.

I'm a 'Telegraph' man myself, but here's a pound. Not much, but if every 'Telegraph' reader sent you a pound the fight against the trouble-makers would be funded for another month.

Good luck!

Never give in!

Yours sincerely,

Henry Root.

Times Newspapers Limited

Registered office: P.O. Box no. 7, New Printing House Square
Gray's Inn Road, London WC1X 8EZ.

Henry Root, Esq.
139 Elm Park Mansions
Park Walk
London, SW10.   April 23rd, 1979

Dear Mr. Root,

Thank you so much for your letter of April 18th, and particularly for the £1 note which I am giving to our Widows and Orphans Fund.

We are fighting as hard as we can and we do not intend to give in.

With all good wishes.

Yours sincerely,

M. J. Hussey
Chief Executive and
Managing Director

139 Elm Park Mansions
Park Walk
London, S.W.10.

C. James Anderton Q.P.M., F.B.I.M.
Chester House,
Boyer Street,
Manchester M16 0RE.   19th April 1979.

Dear Chief Constable,

   I am so sorry not to have replied sooner to your letter
of 27th March. Mrs Root and I are naturally
disappointed that you're unable to address a meeting of
'The Ordinary Folk Against Porn Society', but we quite
understand that you're flat to the boards chasing porno
merchants off your patch. Well done!

   Don't worry about this, because I've had an idea!
We'll come to you!

   Would Tuesday 8th May be convenient? If so we'll
muster in your office at, say, four pm on that day.
There'll just be a handfull of us: myself and Mrs Root,
Major Dewdrop, Dr Littlewinkle and his good lady, the
Snipes (Fred and Rita) together with their youngsters,
Molly (17) and Bruce (19) and the Smithsons.

   We wouldn't want you to go to any trouble on our
behalf, so please don't lay on much of a show. A cup of
tea (Indian please) and some rock cakes would be just
fine. I certainly don't want to eat into funds that would
be better employed putting pimps in the pokey so I

enclose a pound to cover the cost of any hospitality you arrange.

Bring back the rope!

Your pal in the soft south!

Henry Root.

P.S. Please let me know if you can't make it on the arranged date. I'd hate to run into your office with my party only to find you'd sugared off early to play golf with the Lord Mayor!

C James Anderton Q.P.M., F.B.I.M.

Chief Constable

Chief Constable's Office
P O Box 22 (S. West PDO)
Chester House
Boyer Street
Manchester M16 0RE

23rd April 1979.

Dear Mr Root,

I have your letter of 19th April but regret I am not available to meet you as you suggest on Tuesday, 8th May. I am sorry about this.

I doubt if it will be possible for me to meet you and your friends under such arrangements as my busy professional life makes it virtually impossible for me to guarantee such relatively informal contacts. I hope you will understand.

I am returning the £1.00 note you forwarded with your letter.

Yours sincerely,

Chief Constable

H. Root, Esq.,
139 Elm Park Mansions,
Park Walk,
London, S.W.10.

139 Elm Park Mansions
Park Walk
London, S.W.10.

Patrick Moore Esq,
Selsey,
West Sussex.   19th April 1979.

Dear Mr Moore,

I was most interested to read in 'The Sun' yesterday
about the formation of The United Country Party.

I'm not entirely sure that astrologers like yourself
should get mixed up in the real world of politics, but I
like the sound of your platform. (I hope it's a strong one!
Let's face it, you're no feather-weight!) At least you
won't have to rely on the opinion polls to tell you how
you're doing. You'll be able to read it in the stars! Not
that I believe in any of this astrology nonsense. We're
very sceptical, we Capricorns!

The aims of your party sound sensible. Abolish
income tax, clear the rubbish from the streets and crack
down hard on the Welsh. Just what the doctor ordered.
I take it you're in favour of the immediate re-
introduction of hanging?

I'd be most grateful if you could send me a copy of
your manifesto and also if you could let me know
whether you're putting up a candidate in this
constituency (Chelsea) for whom I can vote.

Yours for Law and Order!

Henry Root.

Secretarial Address:
39 West Street,
Selsey, Sussex

Dear Mr. Root,

I hasten to stress that I am an astronomer, not an astrologer! –

Details of manifesto enclosed. Hanging is not on our manifesto, as we feel that this is a matter for everyone's own conscience. I am not a 'hanger' myself, but I believe most people are, and we'd prefer a free vote.

We are campaigning hard here.

All good wishes.

Sincerely

Patrick Moore

139 Elm Park Mansions
Park Walk
London, S.W.10.

Mr Nigel Dempsey,
The Daily Mail,
Carmelite House,
London, E.C.4.   19th April 1979.

Dear Dempsey,

May I say how much I have enjoyed your 'Diary' over the years? Some folk deride sycophantic gossip about one's social superiors as a lot of snobbish nonsense, but I am not of their number. Born, like you, without the advantages, I have acquired, like you, a healthy respect for my 'betters'. I have seen you described in some pseudo-intellectual magazine as having the morals of a cocktail waitress. So what? It happens to be the case that Mrs Root was a cocktail waitress when I met her and not once has she caused me to rue the day I plucked her off her bar-stool and made an honest woman of her.

I write to you now on a matter of some delicacy, but I'm sure I can rely on your discretion. The excellent firm of Jonathan Cape, of whom you may have heard, are shortly to publish my first novel, 'Day of Reckoning', and I am naturally eager that it should receive maximum media exposure.

I'm not some young idealist with his head in the literary clouds, but, like you, a down-to-earth businessman, and I haven't climbed to the top in fish without discovering that you don't get anywhere in life without – how shall I put this? – 'taking care of' a few influential people on the way. I expect you have found this out for yourself.

I now enclose a fiver on the understanding that you will write flatteringly about me when the book appears, linking my name with starlets and suggesting I'm intimate with Barry Sheene and his lady-friend 'Hotpants' Burbank. (I don't have to teach you your business.)

This is only the start. There's plenty more where this came from, so you be good to me and I'll see you're all right!

If you need some background information on me, please don't hesitate to let me know. I'm a very busy man but I could squeeze you in for an interview most mornings before 10 am.

I look forward to reading the first item in your column!

Yours sincerely,

Henry Root.

139 Elm Park Mansions
Park Walk
London, S.W.10.

Jonathan Cape Esq,
Jonathan Cape Ltd,
30 Bedford Square,
London, W.C.1.   19th April 1979.

Dear Cape,

      DAY OF RECKONING by HENRY ROOT.

   I'm told you're always on the alert for solid yarns with
no unnecessary thrills, so I am now enclosing the
synopsis of my recently completed first novel as above.

   Let me say at the outset that the 'property' comes to
you with certain advantages. For the right return on
capital outlay, I'm prepared to help with the financing
of the caper (mainly to ensure maximum media
exposure – your people couldn't get a plug for a bath,
I'm told!) and I have taken the precaution of 'fixing'
certain journalists and literary editors. Nigel Dempsey
of 'The Daily Mail', for instance, is 'in my pocket'.

   An additional advantage is that I shape up brand new
in public, come across well on camera (or so I was told
after being interviewed on a street-corner by Esther
Rantzen on the hilarious topic of, as she put it, 'getting
your leg over the Mrs of a Saturday night') and I'm fully
available with matching luggage to undertake
'exploitation' tours – though not of Turkey, Greece or
Scandinavia.

   Before I accept your offer, I should warn you that
from a business point of view I didn't just fall off a

turnip truck. I'm looking for a heavy advance as a guarantee that you aren't just messing me about. I've heard of too many young writers for whom an offer from a publisher turned out to be a stepping-stone to obscurity.

   Let's go!

Yours sincerely,

Henry Root.

Enc: Synopsis of DAY OF RECKONING by HENRY ROOT.

DAY OF RECKONING

by

HENRY ROOT.

Synopsis

Bronzed, attractive, amazingly fit, 45-year-old Harry Toor, Chairman and Managing Director of Harry Toor Wet Fish Ltd, woke up in the sumptuously appointed bedroom of his luxury mansion in Maidenhead.

He stirred contentedly and, as was usual when he woke, he ran over in his mind his many blessings and possessions: his swimming-pool and tennis courts, his musical cocktail-cabinet and three-piece lounge-room suite in Victoria plum velvet with old-gold lurex edgings (a wedding present from his good mate and next-door neighbour, Michael Parkinson), his Rolls, his expense account trips to Paris, Geneva and New York, his yacht in Monte Carlo, his constant supply of willing 'personal secretaries' and, above all, his latest 'companion', the long-legged, full-bosomed 'starlet', Lorraine Pumptit.

Suddenly he felt strangely ill at ease. Into his mind had come a vision of Barnsley and the back-street slum in which he'd been born and in which his 82-year-old dad and 80-year-old mum still lived. He hadn't visited them in over twenty years. Had it all been worthwhile, his ruthless drive to the top? Did he still know who he was? If he was to visit his old mum and dad now, sample once again his old mum's apple-pie and Yorkshire pudding, play darts with his old dad at the pub on the corner, would he still be able to talk to them, really communicate?

He thought of the little house in which he'd been born, of his old mum and dad, of the lads at the local pork-pie factory who had once been his mates, and of little Janet Gibbens with whom he'd had his first fumbling sexual experience in the back row of the Odeon and he thought:

"Stuff that lot. I'll stay put."

And he went contentedly back to sleep.

THE END

Henry Root
139 Elm Park Mansions
Park Walk
London, S.W.7.

Jonathan Cape Limited

Thirty Bedford Square
London W.C.1

Mr Henry Root,
139 Elm Park Mansions,
Park Walk,
London, S.W.10.   20th April, 1979

Dear Mr Root,

Thank you for your letter of 19th April and synopsis.
We regret that we do not think it would be worth your
while submitting your typescript DAY OF
RECKONING to us, as we do not feel that the book
would be entirely suited to our list.

Please find your synopsis enclosed.

Yours sincerely,

Debra Byron,
Editorial.

Daily Mail

Carmelite House
London, EC4Y 0JA

Mr. H. Root,
139 Elm Park Mansions,
Park Walk,
London, S.W. 10.   20 April, 1979.

Dear Mr. Root,

Thank you for your letter dated 19 April which Mr. Dempster has passed to me.

It is not Mr. Dempster's habit, or that of any other member of the Daily Mail staff, to accept money, or anything else, on the understanding that stories will be written. In the circumstances I return your £5.

Yours sincerely,

GORDON COWAN
Assistant Managing Editor

139 Elm Park Mansions
Park Walk
London, S.W.10.

Mr Gordon Cowan,
The Daily Mail,
Carmelite House,
London, E.C.4.   22nd April 1979.

Dear Mr Cowan,

Thank you for your letter of 20th April in reply to my letter of 19th April to Mr Nigel Dempster.

Why can't he answer his own letters? I was addressing myself to the monkey, not the organ-grinder. Is it the function of an Assistant Managing Editor to act as secretary to the paper's scandal writer? If so, what does the Managing Editor do? The Snooker Correspondent's typing?

Perhaps Mr Dempster will answer this letter. Or does Mr English deal with your mail? It's all very confusing.

Pending an explanation, I return the fiver.

Yours sincerely,

Henry Root.

Daily Mail

Carmelite House
London, EC4Y 0JA.

Mr. H. Root,
139 Elm Park Mansions,
Park Walk,
London, S.W.10.   2 May, 1979

Dear Mr. Root,

Thank you for your further letter dated April 22.

Whatever you may think about newspaper production,
or whatever you may expect, the only
acknowledgement you will receive in this matter is from
me. Mr. Dempster quite rightly brought it to my
attention as the person in charge of editorial
administrations.

You have now received the courtesy of two letters on
the matter and I consider this correspondence closed. I
return to you your money and reiterate that we do not
accept money from anyone on the understanding that
stories will be written about them.

Yours sincerely,

GORDON COWAN
Assistant Managing Editor

139 Elm Park Mansions
Park Walk
London, S.W.10.

Mr Brian Clough,
'The Boss!',
Nottingham Forest F.C.,
Nottingham.   23rd March 1979.

Dear Mr Clough,

So you stuffed the Swiss! Magic! Mustard! You and
the lads must be over the moon!

I was a bit disturbed by a pre-match report in my
paper that you were thinking of buying their big striker,
Sulser. The lad looks useful (you must have been as sick
as a parrot when he stuck the ball in the back of the net
to make it none one against you!) but where would this
leave the boy Birtles? On top of which, is it possible for a
foreign player to familiarise himself with the English
way of doing things? You know what I mean. I'm
talking about being a credit to the game on and off the
field. Short hair, smart appearance, train hard, no
cussing or monkey-business in the changing-room and
just one holiday a year with the wife and kiddies in
Majorca.

Now, Henry Root's no snitch, but I think you ought
to know that at half-time against the Grasshoppers,
Archie Gemmill ('The Wee Man') blew his nose onto
the pitch. Surely this isn't the Notts Forest way? I think
you should remind your players that when they're on
TV they are guests in our lounge-rooms and the last
thing we want to see is them blowing their noses onto
the lounge-room floor.

Anyway, here's a pound towards Sulser's fee. In

spite of my reservations as expressed above, I recognise that you're the boss and that what you say goes.

You'll never walk alone!

Yours ever,

Henry Root.

139 Elm Park Mansions
Park Walk
London, S.W.10.

Mr Brian Clough,
'The Boss',
Nottingham Forest F.C.,
Nottingham.   23rd April 1979.

Dear Mr Clough,

Did you get my letter of 23rd March, enclosing a pound for the boy Sulser? Since you don't strike me as being the sort of man who'd pocket a pound without so much as a 'ta very much, lad', I assume my letter must have gone astray. In the circumstances, here's another pound. Let me know if this one doesn't arrive either.

Now – about the return with Cologne. I've got a daring suggestion to make. Drop the Big Man, Shilton! Let's face it, he failed to dominate 'the box' in the first leg and I ask myself whether he's got the bottle for the big occasion. Remember what happened in the World Cup against Poland? Perhaps in preferring Clemence, Mr Greenwood is turning out to be less stupid than he looks.

As for the two big centre-backs, well, one of them's got to go. Why don't you buy Toddy? I don't have to tell you of all people that he's still the most cultured No 6 in the world and I see he's now playing in the Everton Reserves, having had no less than sixteen of his majestic lapses in four minutes against West Bromwich last week. You could probably pick him up for a song or swop him for the wild-man Burnsy, *who is not your sort of player*. Some of us haven't forgotten how, against Arsenal last season, he saved a certain goal by knocking the opposing No 9 as cold as a stoat with an Army-surplus sandbag he'd taken with him onto the park. Effective, but not the Notts Forest way.

I'm glad to be able to report that at half-time in the first-leg against Cologne, Archie Gemmill ('The Wee Man') didn't blow his nose onto the pitch or do anything else to bring the game into disrepute. Possibly this was because he wasn't still on the field, having gone crook after a few minutes. I hope he's recovered now. He's a bonny wee fighter and you need him in the side.

Good luck in the return leg!

You're the Boss!

You'll never walk alone!

Your pal in the stands!

Henry Root.

Nottingham Forest Football Club

City Ground
Nottingham NG2 5FJ

Mr. H. Root,
139 Elm Park Mansions,
Park Walk,
London, S.W.10.   24th April, 1979.

Dear Mr. Root,

Thank you for your letters dated 23rd March and 23rd April, and I must apologise for not replying to you sooner, but having spent so much time with the players recently, due to playing four to five games per week, and I have had hardly any time to sit in the office and answer my correspondence. I have had to plough through a pile of over a hundred letters to find your original correspondence, but I can assure you that you would have had a reply in due course.

I am returning the second pound note you sent me, but will put the original one into our "Sulser Fund", and hope that you will not mind us using it for another transfer fee should say, Kevin Keegan, come onto the market first.

Once again, sorry for the delay, but I hope you understand my position.

Yours sincerely,

B. Clough,
Manager.

139 Elm Park Mansions
Park Walk
London, S.W.10.

Mrs Joan Pugh,
London Weekend Television Ltd,
London, S.E.1.   23rd April 1979.

Dear Mrs Pugh,

   I am applying for the job of Programme Researcher in
your new 'Minorities Unit', as advertised in this week's
'Spectator'.

   Don't get me wrong. I've made my pile, I'm semi-
retired and I certainly don't need the work. But I'm glad
to see your company's leading the long over-due
crackdown on the minorities in our society –
homosexuals, immigrants, drug addicts and young
people – and I'd like to support you. Quite frankly,
after such unaffirmative shows as 'The London
Programme' (in which, if Godfrey Hodgson isn't
making hearsay allegations against the Metropolitan
CID, a sharp-nosed young lady called Yvonne Roberts
is poking up back alleys after prostitutes) I'm agreeably
surprised that you're at last taking a responsible line.
Worried about your licence being renewed? Nothing
wrong with that.

   Here are the facts of my life in a nut-shell:

   Born 4th January 1935. Left school at 16 with one 'O'
level in geography (so I know my way around the
world), but continued my education at the University of
Real Life, than which, you will agree, there is none
better.

   From the age of 16 to 18 worked as a porter in

Billingsgate Fish Market. Gained invaluable experience of the English working class's dislike of ethnic minorities and so-called intellectuals. From 18 to 20 did my National Service in submarines under the legendary Captain 'Crap' Myers VC. Commissioned.

On being demobbed, started my own wet fish business. Worked like a black (but paid myself rather better) and was able to sell the business for a tidy sum in 1976. Now find myself with time on my hands. Looking for new challenges with a societal bias.

Personal details: 5ft 8¾ins, 15 stone, English on both sides of the family as far back as can be traced (1904). Expert shot. Front upper denture due to boxing mishap sustained during National Service. (17 fights, 2 convictions.) Married Muriel Root (née Potts) in 1958. Two youngsters – Doreen (19) and Henry Jr (15.)

May I say how much I'm looking forward to joining your team and to flushing out the ethnic woodworms from the fixtures and fittings of our society.

Yours Against Minorities!

Henry Root.

P.S. I don't want to influence your decision one way or another, but I think I ought to tell you that Mr Michael Grade is a personal friend of mine, as the enclosed letter will show.

P.P.S. I'm a bit concerned about your address. Isn't S.E.1. rather out of the picture media-wise? Can you assure me that, located as you are on the wrong side of the river, you don't find yourselves somewhat isolated from where it's happening? I don't want to be stuck up some dead-end back-water.

London Weekend Television

South Bank Television Centre, Kent House, Upper Ground
London SE1 9LT

Henry Root Esq.,
139 Elm Park Mansions,
Park Walk,
London, S.W.10.   29th March, 1979

Dear Mr. Root,

Thank you for your letter.

Yours sincerely,

MICHAEL GRADE
DIRECTOR OF PROGRAMMES

London Weekend Television

South Bank Television Centre, Kent House, Upper Ground
London SE1 9LT

Henry Root, Esq.,
139, Elm Park Mansions,
Park Walk,
London SW10

10th April, 1979

Dear Mr. Root,

Thank you for your letter of the 9th May. I am sorry
that you have not received a reply to your application
for the London Minorities Unit vacancy, but I am afraid
this may take some time as we have had over 600
applications. You will however be notified if you are to
be called for interview or not.

Thank you for your interest.

Yours sincerely,

Mrs. Joan Pugh,
Staff Officer

139 Elm Park Mansions
Park Walk
London, S.W.10.

The Rt Hon William Whitelaw,
Conservative Central Office,
32 Smith Square,
London, S.W.1.   24th April 1979.

Dear Mr Whitelaw,

Following the disgraceful and unprovoked attempt
by left-wing extremists to break up the perfectly lawful
National Front meeting in Southall last night, I was
most relieved to hear you say on 'News at Ten' that you
would make no attempt as Home Secretary (which,
God willing, you soon will be) to ban further National
Front rallies, marches or meetings.

Don't misunderstand me – I'm no supporter of the
Front. The pity is that successive Governments, both
Tory and Labour, have, by weak-kneed policies on
immigration, played into their hands. It remains true,
however, that a citizen has a basic human right to
express his views – however obnoxious these views
may be. That's what we call freedom of speech and it
was reassuring, Sir, to hear you assert this freedom on
the News last night with all the considerable eloquence
at your command.

One thing bothers me, however. You will agree, I
hope, that while every citizen should have the right to
express his opinions openly – however unpleasant and
prejudiced these opinion may be – this right should
not be granted to pornographers.

It is one thing to daub racist slogans in public places,
quite another for sweetshops and newsagents to openly

display photographs of naked ladies where kiddies can see them. You will agree, I think, that our young folk are far more likely to be depraved and corrupted by the latter than by the former.

Can I have your assurance, Sir, that as Home Secretary under Mrs Thatcher, you will do nothing to impede the passage through Parliament of Mr Hugh Rossi's sensible Obscene Displays Act, but that if, say, The National Party of Pornographers and Pederasts tried to hold a meeting in Southall you would stamp down on them with all your considerable weight?

I have two youngsters of my own, Sir, and I can assure you that I would rather they exposed themselves to Mr Enoch Powell than that they should be confronted in their local sweetshop by the naked bosoms of some so-called 'topless model'.

Here's a pound. Use it to enforce law and order!

Yours for Freedom of Speech except for Pornographers!

Henry Root.

Copy to Mr Richard West.

Penrith and The Border Constituency

Parliamentary Election – 1979

Conservative Candidate

Willie Whitelaw

Central Committee Rooms,
31 Chiswick Street, Carlisle.

27th April, 1979

Dear Mr. Root,

Thank you very much for your kind donation to our Conservative Party.

I will always defend free speech in our country although I do equally vehemently oppose extremists who use violence utterly alien to our democratic tradition.

I can confirm that our Conservative Party will take action against pornography. Mr. Rossi's Bill revived legislation which our Government prepared in 1973 but which the present Government ignored on taking power.

Yours sincerely,

Dictated by Mr. Whitelaw
and signed in his absence
by his secretary.

Henry Root, Esq.,
139 Elm Park Mansions,
Park Walk,
London, S.W.10.

Vote Whitelaw

139 Elm Park Mansions
Park Walk
London, S.W.10.

Mr Leslie Crowther,
c/o Thames Television Ltd,
306 Euston Road,
London, N.W.1.   26th April 1979.

Dear Leslie,

Could you settle a dispute between me and Mrs Root?
(You're her favourite comedian – I can't think why! No,
I'm only joking!) Anyway, she holds that you're in your
sixties, but I say that that's impossible unless you've
had your face lifted. But if you *had* had your face lifted
you wouldn't be able to smile all the time like you do
now. Your ears would drop off! I say you're only in your
late fifties. Could you settle this argument for us, once
and for all?

Congratulations on your recent show on Thames! It
was most amusing – good clean entertainment with no
allusions to matters appertaining to the water-works.
(That's rare enough these days, alas.)

Here are a couple of wise-cracks you could use on
your next show. Just give me the credit. Say 'Additional
wise-cracks by Henry Root'. That would be okay.

1. Bob Monkhouse. "You know, Dickie, it's not easy
   making millions of people laugh".
   Dickie Henderson: "Sensible of you never to have
   tried, Bob!"

2. Question. "What's an innuendo?"
   Irish Literary Critic: "An Italian suppository!"

Could you possibly oblige with a photo for Mrs Root?
She'd be really thrilled! I expect you get literally millions
of letters from ordinary folk like me, so I enclose the
postage for your convenience.

You're okay!

Yours,

Henry Root.

Temple Court,
Corston,
Nr. Bath,
Avon.

Dear Henry,

Many thanks for your delicious letter which arrived
in time for breakfast.

Here is the photograph for Mrs. Root – I could not
get one of Bob Monkhouse – which I hope she will like.

Yours sincerely,
Good Luck!!

Leslie Crowther.

139 Elm Park Mansions
Park Walk
London, S.W.10.

General Zia-ut-Haq,
The Strong Man!,
The President's Office,
Islamabad,
Pakistan.   26th April 1979.

Mr President!

In recent weeks you will have read unflattering
reference to yourself in our so-called liberal press. Pay
no attention! Most of us realise that a backward people
such as yours needs, and appreciates, the smack of firm
government.

We are not a backward people, of course, which
makes our sad National Decline in recent years all the
harder for patriots to stomach.

Many take it as the final straw that in Kent – the
garden of England, I might remind you, Sir, – the
county cricket team is currently captained by a dusky
character who rejoices in some such unlikely name as
Asif Iqbal!

Happily for us, Margaret Thatcher – a strong man
like yourself – is about to come to power. As she
stomps the country, invoking the glorious example of
such great Englishmen from our island story as St
Francis Drake and Sir Walter Pidgeon, the streets ring
with the sound of do-gooders breaking wind and taking
to the boats. Some will find a welcome, no doubt, in the
licensed brothels and drug-parlours of Holland and
Denmark, but most will be blown onto the rocks of
obscurity by the hot wind of her rhetoric.

Her first priority – and one which will greatly appeal to you, Mr President – is the immediate restoration of capital punishment, not least for those who have committed murder. There's a long way to go before Britain once again rules the world, of course, but this is a step in the right direction, I think you'll agree.

Could you oblige with a photo, Mr President? It would have pride of place, next to the late lamented Generalissiomo Franco, in my gallery of great International Conservatives.

You're all right!

Yours respectfully,

Henry Root.

The Islamic Republic of Pakistan

General M. Zia-ul-Haq

Islamabad

06 May 79

Henry Root, Esq
139 Elm Park Mansions
Park Walk
London, S.W. 10
U.K.

Dear Mr Root,

Thank you for your letter of 26 April 79.

I appreciate your thoughtfulness in writing to me to convey certain very pertinent views.

Enclosed is my photograph which you have requested. I have also signed it.

Wishing you all the best,

Yours sincerely,

General
(M. Zia-ul-Haq)

Ms Audrey Whiting,
Royal Correspondent!
The Sunday Mirror,
Holborn Circus,
London, E.C.1.   30th April 1979.

Dear Ms Whiting,

I was deeply shocked to read your article in yesterday's 'Sunday Mirror' about the acute shortage of 'Royals' and the consequent strain on Her Majesty the Queen.

I have a suggestion to make. We now have Life Peers. Would it not be sensible to apply this concept to the creation of Life Royals?

I have in mind folk of the utmost probity, folk who, like Her Majesty, are above the rough and tumble of mere politics, folk who have swum resolutely against the tide of declining morality over the past years and have managed, like Her Majesty, to affirm the traditional values and family virtues in all they've done.

I'm talking about people such as Group Captain Sir Douglas 'Hang 'em all' Bader, Miss Mary Kenny, Mr John Junor, Dr J. P. R. Williams, Mr Bobby Charlton, Sir Richard Attenborough, Sir 'John' Mills, Dame Ninette de Neagle, Miss Nanette Newman, Mr Laurie McMenemy ('The Big Man!'), Mary O'Hara the dancing nun from Glasgow (to keep the Scots in their place) and Ms Val Doonican (ditto the Welsh.)

You will notice that not all these people are from what

[111]

might be called 'the top drawer'. But the same could be said, let's face it, of some of our present Royals. The criteria for being a Life Royal should have nothing to do with 'class' as such. Life Royals, like actual Royals, should be ordinary, but exceptional, folk up whom lesser folk will naturally look but with whom they can relate.

What do you think?

Yours sincerely,

Henry Root.

Copies to:

Her Majesty the Queen.
Miss Mary Kenny.
Mr John Junor.

139 Elm Park Mansions
Park Walk
London, S.W.10.

Her Majesty the Queen,
Buckingham Palace,
London, S.W.1.   30th April 1979.

Your Majesty,

   I enclose a copy of a letter I have sent to Ms Audrey
Whiting, 'The Sunday Mirror's' Royal Authority.

   I was most shocked to read Ms Whiting's article about
the reluctance of certain members of your family to
attend Royal Occasions of the sort that Lord Delfont
keeps arranging for you and I think my concept of Life
Royals might be the answer. (What a shame,
incidentally, that I couldn't include Lord Delfont
among my suggested candidates for enroyalment. He
would have been ideal, but by creating him a Life Peer,
Sir Harold Wilson foolishly rendered him unviable.)

   I was so sorry to read about the trouble you're having
with Princess Anne. My Doreen (19) is off the rails too,
so I know what it's like.

   Could you oblige me with a photo, Ma'am? I'd be
very honoured.

Your humble subject,

Henry Root.

Copy to: Miss Mary Kenny.

Fleet Street, London

1st May 1979

Dear Mr. Root,

Thank you very much for having sent me a copy of your letter to the Sunday Mirror.

I am greatly flattered by your nomination of me as a "Life Royal". But I very much doubt if the Royal Family would find me an acceptable substitute!

With all good wishes,

Yours sincerely,

JOHN JUNOR

Henry Root Esq.,
139, Elm Park Mansions,
Park Walk,
London, S.W.10.

BUCKINGHAM PALACE

10th May, 1979.

Dear Mr. Root,

I am commanded by The Queen to write and thank you for your letter and enclosure, the contents of which have been noted.

In answer to your request for a photograph of Her Majesty, I have to explain to you that owing to The Queen's rules in these matters, it is not possible to do as you ask.

When I tell you of the many similar requests that Her Majesty receives, I feel sure you will understand the reason for these rules and that The Queen would not wish to break them for one and not for others.

Yours sincerely,

Lady-in-Waiting

Henry Root Esq.,
139 Elm Park Mansions,
Park Walk,
London, S.W.1.

The Prime Minister! (Mrs Margaret Thatcher!)
10 Downing Street,
London, S.W.1.   4th May 1979.

Dear Prime Minister!

Congratulations! We did it! What a day! History has been made!

Enough of that. As you said when you arrived at No 10 this afternoon: "There's work to be done."

That's right. It's straight down to business. (Don't worry! There'll be plenty of time later for women's work like measuring for new curtains!) We've got to form a Cabinet of hard-nosed men to prosecute our number 1 priority: the crackdown on the unions, the work-shy, law-breakers and homosexuals. I hope there won't be too many 'Oxbridge' men in our Cabinet. Dragged from the lecture-room into real life, they have trouble, in my experience, in discovering what day of the week it is. I'd like to make three suggestions:

1. For Home Secretary – Mrs Whitehouse. The self-appointed intellectuals sneer at her, but she's a mother like yourself. I read recently in 'The Sun' of how she visited you in your room at the House and how you showed each other pornographic pictures and knelt of the floor and prayed together. That was moving.

2. For Minister of Defence – Laurie McMenemy. As you may know he's the manager of Southampton FC at the moment, but he's got the shoulders to shine on a wider stage than the green turf of Wembley.

Southampton have played in Europe, so he's had invaluable experience of 'kicking the foreigners into the stands'. I assume he's a Tory, but I'm writing to him on your behalf to check. I certainly never saw a Socialist with a back as straight as his.

3. For 'Our Man in Europe' – Paul Johnson. All right! All right! So they say he's a carrot-haired loony! So they call him Colonel 'Bonkers' Johnson! So what? Have they forgotten General Wolfe, the victor at Quebec? He was as mad as a hatter but he sent the Frogs packing! Johnson said to my father once:

"Root! You and I are old enough to remember a time when you could walk from one end of the Champs Elysées to the other without seeing a Frenchman! Those were the days!"

Johnson won't let you down, but watch out for the softies in the party. I don't care for the look of Norman St John Stevas. My father taught me two things I've never forgotten.

"Mind this, son," he used to say. "Never spit in a man's face unless his moustache is on fire. And never trust a man who wears mauve underpants at tea-time."

I don't think we should have any bachelors in our Cabinet unless it's entirely necessary.

Here's a pound!

Bring back the rope! Let's go!

Your man on the door-step!

Henry Root.

Copies to: Mr Laurie McMenemy, Mr Paul Johnson and Mrs Whitehouse.

10 DOWNING STREET

10th May 1979

Dear Mr Root,

The Prime Minister has asked me to thank you very much for your kind letter of 4th May. Your message of congratulations is greatly appreciated and thank you very much for sending us another £1 for our Party funds.

With best wishes.

Richard Ryder
Political Office

Henry Root Esq.

SOUTHAMPTON FOOTBALL CLUB LIMITED

The Dell, Milton Road,
Southampton SO9 4XX.

16th May 1979.

Dear Mr. Root,

Thank you for your considerations and I am very flattered that you put my name forward to Mrs. Thatcher. Should she decide to call on me perhaps you could let me know as soon as possible before I make too many plans for next season!

Seriously, I think she must have chosen her Cabinet by now and, like yourself, I do hope she does a good job.

Best wishes.

Yours sincerely,

L. McMenemy,
Manager.

The First Sea Lord,
The Admiralty,
Whitehall,
London, S.W.1.

17th April 1979.

My Lord,

I was alarmed to read a recent article in 'The Spectator' by Mrs Thatcher's chiropodist, Dr Patrick Cosgrave, concerning the imminent outbreak of hostilities with the Soviets.

Has a definite date been fixed? Mrs Root is pressing me to take her on a sun-shine holiday for two to the Canary Isles, but as an ex-serving officer I naturally don't want to be out of the country when the balloon goes up.

I may say that in the performance of my National Service it was my pleasure to be under the legendary Captain 'Crap' Myers VC in the Med. He it was, as you'll remember, who during the last show took a Bolshie rating onto the casing of his submarine and shot him as dead as a skunk — or so the story goes.

I'm on red alert here and can leave for my ship at the drop of a bollard, but I shall need to know where to go and how to interpret my coded orders. No point in ex-serving officers all over the country receiving a telegram from the Admiralty reading: "Pigshit! Scuttle!" and not being able to decipher it.

I am awaiting your signal, my Lord.

Let's not have a cock-up like last time!

Yours for the defence of this once great country!

Henry Root. (Ex-Sub Lt, RNVR.)

P.S. I know what Navy efficiency is like so I am enclosing a stamp to expedite the promulgation of my orders.

NO REPLY!

139 Elm Park Mansions
Park Walk
London, S.W.10.

The Rt Hon Francis Pym,
The Ministry of Defence,
Whitehall,
London, S.W.1.   8th May 1979.

Dear Mr Pym,

May I say how much more easily in our beds we
ordinary folk will sleep now that we once again have a
Minister of Defence ready to stand up to the Soviets?

Tourist in Whitehall: "Excuse me, can you tell me
which side the War Office is on?"
Englishman: "Ours, I hope."
A joke, possibly, but not, you will agree, a very funny
one.

On 17th April, having read an article in 'The
Spectator' by Mrs Thatcher's chiropodist, Dr Patrick
Cosgrave, about the imminent outbreak of hostilities
with the Warsaw Pact countries, I wrote to the First Sea
Lord alerting him to my availability and requesting
information as to what would be the signal telling me to
join my ship (I am an ex-submarine officer.)

To my amazement, I received no reply! Under a
Socialist Government it was not so surprising, I
suppose, that we would once again have been up the
creek, due to those in charge of our affairs having been
caught with their trousers down.

You, Sir, will change all this, I know. I would be most
grateful if you would look into this matter for me and let

me know why ordinary folk like me, prepared to fight for our country, should be treated with such high-handed contempt by the authorities.

I look forward to hearing from you, Sir.

Stand up for our country!

Support the Iron Lady!

Yours for a good scrap,

Henry Root.

Ministry of Defence

Old Admiralty Building Spring Gardens London SW1A 2BE

H Root Esq
139 Elm Park Mansions
Park Walk
LONDON SW10

Date 16 May 1979

Dear Mr Root

The Secretary of State for Defence has asked me to
thank you for your encouraging letter of 8 May and I am
to inform you that your willingness to serve in the Royal
Navy in the event of hostilities has been noted.

I can assure you that no slight was intended by the
delay in answering your earlier letter and you should
shortly receive a reply from the Office of the First Sea
Lord.

Yours faithfully

G W OWENS

From: Captain W. A. Higgins, Royal Navy

Secretary to First Sea Lord

Ministry of Defence

Main Building, Whitehall, London SW1A 2HB

No. 3300/13/2   16th May 1979.

Dear Mr Root,

First Sea Lord was most grateful for your letter of 17th April offering your services should hostilities break out and he has asked me to pass on his thanks. However, in view of your age I am sorry to say that there is no prospect of us being able to employ you in the Reserves despite your earlier service.

I hope you will be relieved to learn that we have no reason to believe that war is imminent but the only sure way to deter any possible Soviet adventurism in the future is by keeping our defences well up. The fact that our Government intends to do this is surely emphasised by the prominence given to Defence in yesterday's Queen's Speech.

Yours sincerely

Bill Higgins

Henry Root, Esq.

139 Elm Park Mansions
Park Walk
London, S.W.10.

Lord Hailsham,
The House of Lords,
London, S.W.1.   8th May 1979.

My Lord,

   May I say what a great pleasure it is to have once
again a man with a broad bottom on the woolsack?

   May I also say what a relief it is to ordinary folk such
as myself to have a Lord Chancellor with some
determination to uphold Law and Order?

   As the enclosed letter will show, I wrote to your
Socialist predecessor on 28th March on a matter of great
public concern. It was naive of me, perhaps, to expect a
reply. While expressing a safe, generalised concern for
the common man when canvassing his vote, Socialists,
in my experience, treat him individually with the
utmost contempt, ignoring, when they come to power,
his hopes, his fears, his worries and his desires.

   I know that you, my Lord, are a public servant of a
very different kidney, and I look forward to hearing that
you, unlike your uncaring predecessor, will be taking
strong action in this disgraceful episode concerning
Judge Joseph Zigmund (sic) and this country's finest
policeman, Mr James Anderton.

   Bring back the rope!

   Yours faithfully,

   Henry Root.

Enc: Letter dated 28/3/79 to the Lord Chancellor.

139 Elm Park Mansions
Park Walk,
London, S.W.1.

The Lord Chancellor,
The House of Lords,
London, S.W.1.   28th March 1979.

My Lord,

As an ordinary member of the public, I must protest
in the strongest possible terms at the unwarranted
rebuke Mr James Anderton (the Chief Constable of
Manchester and this country's finest policeman) and
his devoted body of men recently received from so-
called Judge Joseph Zigmund.

Allow me, my Lord, to remind you of the relevant
details. After much diligent police work (which
involved fifty of Manchester's best detectives lurking
for an irksome nine months in a public house, when
they might have been more amusingly employed
picking prostitutes off the streets, raiding family
newsagents in search of offensive materials and visiting
so-called massage parlours) a Mrs Lillian Semmonds
(sic) was brought before the court, accused of the vile
offence of controlling a prostitute.

Fining her a derisory £50, the Judge proceeded to tell
the police that they had been wasting everyone's time
and then observed that the prostitute and Mrs
Semmonds had anyway been enjoying a lesbian
relationship! As though that mitigated the offence!

As you will agree, my Lord, this evil woman should
have received a five year prison sentence for controlling
a prostitute and another five years (to run
consecutively) for being a lesbian.

Who is this Judge Joseph Zigmund? Why doesn't he practise law in his own country? Is it a consequence of our joining the Common Market that foreigners are now allowed to preside over our courts?

With the greatest respect, my Lord, I await your explanation and to hearing what action you are taking to punish Judge Joseph Zigmund and to defend the good name of Mr James Anderton: a man who has been compared (by himself) to Christ and who, single-handed, is engaged on the lonely task of combatting the forces of darkness.

Yours faithfully,

Henry Root.

139 Elm Park Mansions
Park Walk
London, S.W.10.

s Esther Rantzen,
    That's Life',
elevision Centre,
London, W.12.

23rd April 1979.

Dear Esther,
    You're a fat idiot and your show's a disgrace.
    Yours sincerely,

Henry Root

Henry Root.

BRITISH BROADCASTING CORPORATION
KENSINGTON HOUSE RICHMOND WAY LONDON W14 0AX
TELEGRAMS AND CABLES: TELECASTS LONDON TELEX
TELEPHONE 01-743 1272   TELEX 265781
BBC tv

REF: SLER

26/4/79

Dear Mr. Root,
    Thank you very much indeed for taking the trouble to
write to me. Hearing from viewers like yourself is a
tremendous morale boost for us all - it really makes a
great difference to me to know that you find our work
enjoyable and worthwhile. May I send you my best wishes,
and thank you again for your letter.

    Yours sincerely,

Esther Rantzen

139 Elm Park Mansions
Park Walk
London, S.W.10.

Major-General Wyldbore-Smith, C.B., D.S.O., O.B.E.,
Conservative Board of Finance,
32 Smith Square,
Westminster,
London, S.W.1.

7th August 1979.

Dear Major-General Wyldbore-Smith,

I'm a blunt man, accustomed to plain-speaking, so I'll come straight to the point.

What's the going price for getting an honour?

I'm not talking about an M.B.E., an O.B.E. or a C.B.E. They seem to be for ballet dancers, disc-jockeys, crooners and those who are quick over the high hurdles. (No offence meant. I see that you yourself have the O.B.E. Nothing wrong with that. Well done!) No, I'm talking about a life peerage, or, at the very least, a knighthood like my friend Sir James Goldsmith.

In the course of the past year I have contributed steadily and generously to Tory Party funds. Your understrapper Brigadier L.H. Lee C.B.E. will confirm this. (I am writing to you rather than him, incidentally, because you seem to outrank him and because you have the more sensible name.) I realise, however, that I will have to think in terms of a rather more substantial lump sum in order to secure a place near the top of Mrs Thatcher's New Year hand-outs.

Can you give me an idea of the approximate amount?

I read recently that a 'drop' of as little as £25,000 to one of our leading politicians was enough to obtain a seat in the Lords for the donor.

Has inflation bumped up the price?

Let me know. I'm waiting here with my cheque-book ready!

Support Mrs Thatcher!

Yours sincerely,

Henry Root

Henry Root.

P.S. It goes without saying that there could be 'something in this' for you personally.

CONSERVATIVE BOARD OF FINANCE

Chairman:
R. ALISTAIR McALPINE

Director:
MAJOR-GENERAL F.B. WYLDBORE-SMITH,
C.B., D.S.O., O.B.E.

Deputy Director:
BRIGADIER L.H. LEE, C.B.E.

32 SMITH SQUARE,
WESTMINSTER. SW1P 3HH

TELEPHONE: 01-222 9000

14th August 1979

Henry Root Esq.,
139 Elm Park Mansions
Park Walk
<u>London SW10</u>

Dear Mr. Root,

Thank you for your letter of the 7th August. I think I must make it absolutely clear that there is no question of buying Honours from the Conservative Party.

However, I am most grateful to you for the support which you have given to the Party over the past few months.

Yours sincerely,

F.B. Wyldbore-Smith

139 Elm Park Mansions
Park Walk
London, S.W.10.

H.R.H. The Prince of Wales,
c/o Buckingham Palace, (please forward)
London, S.W.1.   18th May 1979.

Your Royal Highness,

        Inspired by the example of your uncle, Lord Mountbatten, I
have decided to throw my flat open to the public on Saturday 9th
June.

        I reckon to pull in the Japs and the more gullible of our
American friends. The idea is to show them how an _ordinary_ English
couple lives.

        I'll take the mugs on a conducted tour of the premises while
Mrs Root and my two youngsters, Doreen (19) and Henry Jr (15), continue doing what any average family does at weekends: that is to
say stretching the family budget by bottling plums, lolling about
painting one's finger-nails and carrying out the weekly bullworker
maintenance. Mrs Root will be bottling plums, Doreen will be oiling
her bullworker and Henry Jr will be painting his finger-nails, but
that's young people these days.

        Would you consider performing the opening ceremony? We'd be
very honoured and it would be nice for you to meet my Doreen. If
you found yourself a little short, I'd be prepared, like your uncle
Lord Mountbatten, to sock you the pound entrance fee till you
straightened up.

        I look forward to hearing from you, Sir.

        Support Mrs Thatcher!

        Yours respectfully,

        Henry Root

        Henry Root. A naval man like yourself!

PS.   Sorry to send this care of Her Majesty, but you don't seem
to be in the phone book.

BUCKINGHAM PALACE

From: The Assistant Private Secretary to H.R.H. The Prince of Wales

4th June, 1979

Dear Mr Root

The Prince of Wales has asked me to thank you very much for your letter to him of 18th May in which you asked if he would be able to visit your flat on Saturday 9th June.

I am afraid His Royal Highness will be unable to accept your kind invitation since he has already made his plans for that day.

Yours Sincerely

Oliver Everett

Oliver Everett

Henry Root, Esq.

139 Elm Park Mansions
Park Walk
London, S.W.10.

The Lucie Clayton Model Agency,
168 Brompton Road,
London, S.W.1.

9th April 1979.

Dear Sir or Madame,

Once a year the officers and men of the Rifle Brigade meet to discuss old times in the course of a knees-up. Yours truly is the Organising Secretary of this year's get-together which is to be held in a private suite at the Savoy Hotel on Friday 25th May.

I'd like you to supply the cabaret. What we have in mind are a dozen or so 'models' to jump out of a cake and 'mingle' with the guests.

I naturally don't want to be too explicit in a letter, but perhaps I should emphasise that the 'models' should be top types and would be expected to 'go a bit', if you follow me.

We would be prepared to pay each girl a minimum of £100 for the evening's work, and no girl would be required to 'go with' more than six officers or two men.

I look forward to doing business with you.

Yours sincerely,

Henry Root

Henry Root.

168 Brompton Road London SW3 1HW   01-581 0024

LUCIE CLAYTON

4th May 1979

Henry Root Esq
139 Elm Park Mansions
LONDON SW10

Dear Mr Root

Neither the Savoy Hotel, nor the adjutant
of your former regiment, confirm your statement about the 25th May and certainly you
are writing to the wrong agency. I have,
however, been on to the Provost-Marshal's
department who will be sending some men
to see what it is that you really need.

Yours sincerely

S Neill
REGISTRAR

LUCIE CLAYTON LIMITED
Directors: Lucie Clayton   Ann Bridges   Cecilia Lumley   Leslie Kark M.A ·Oxon·, FRSA ·Chairman·

50 Years
FOUNDED 1928

The Registrar,
Lucie Clayton, Ltd,
168 Brompton Road,
London, S.W.3.

139 Elm Park Mansions
Park Walk
London, S.W.10.

5th May 1979.

Dear Miss Neill,
I don't understand. It was the Provost Marshal who recommended
you in the first place.
Yours sincerely,

Henry Root
Henry Root.

139 Elm Park Mansions
Park Walk
London, S.W.10.

General Zia-ut-Haq,
The Strong Man!,
The President's Office,
Islamabad,
Pakistan.   26th April 1979.

Mr President!

    In recent weeks you will have read unflattering reference
to yourself in our so-called liberal press. Pay no attention!
Most of us realise that a backward people such as yours needs,
and appreciates, the smack of firm government.

    We are not a backward people, of course, which makes our
sad National Decline in recent years all the harder for patriots
to stomach.

    Many take it as the final straw that in Kent - the garden
of England, I might remind you, Sir, - the county cricket team
is currently captained by a dusky character who rejoices in some
such unlikely name as Asif Iqbal!

    Happily for us, Margaret Thatcher - a strong man like your-
self - is about to come to power. As she stomps the country, invoking the glorious example of such great Englishman from our
island story as St Francis Drake and Sir Walter Pidgeon, the streets
ring with the sound of do-gooders breaking wind and taking to the
boats. Some will find a welcome, no doubt, in the licensed brothels
and drug-parlours of Holland and Denmark, but most will be blown
onto the rocks of obscurity by the hot wind of her rhetoric.

    Her first priority - and one which will greatly appeal to
you, Mr President - is the immediate restoration of capital punishment, not least for those who have committed murder. There's
a long way to go before Britain once again rules the world, of
course, but this is a step in the right direction, I think you'll
agree.

    Could you oblige with a photo, Mr President? It would have
pride of place, next to the late lamented Generalissimo Franco, in
my gallery of great International Conservatives.

    You're all right!

    Yours respectfully,

    Henry Root

    Henry Root.

بِسْمِ اللَّهِ الرَّحْمَٰنِ الرَّحِيمِ

THE ISLAMIC REPUBLIC OF PAKISTAN

General M. Zia-ul-Haq

Henry Root, Esq
139 Elm Park Mansions
Park Walk
London, S.W. 10
U.K.

Dean Mr Root,

Thank you for your letter of 26 April 79.

I appreciate your thoughtfulness in writing to me to convey certain very pertinent views.

Enclosed is my photograph which you have requested. I have also signed it.

Wishing you all the best,

Yours sincerely,

General
(M. Zia-ul-Haq)

Root, with my
and very best wishes
Zia ul

139 Elm Park Mansions
Park Walk
London, S.W.10.

The Prime Minister! (Mrs Margaret Thatcher!)
10 Downing Street,
London, S.W.1.   4th May 1979.

Dear Prime Minister!

        Congratulations! We did it! What a day! History has been made!

        Enough of that. As you said when you arrived at No 10 this afternoon: "There's work to be done."

        That's right. It's straight down to business. (Don't worry! There'll be plenty of time later for women's work like measuring for new curtains!) We've got to form a Cabinet of hard-nosed men to prosecute our number 1 priority: the crackdown on the unions, the work-shy, law-breakers and homosexuals. I hope there won't be too many 'Oxbridge' men in our Cabinet. Dragged from the lecture-room into real life, they have trouble, in my experience, in discovering what day of the week it is. I'd like to make three suggestions:

        1. For Home Secretary - Mrs Whitehouse. The self-appointed intellectuals sneer at her, but she's a mother like yourself. I read recently in 'The Sun' of how she visited you in your room at the House and how you showed each other pornographic pictures and knelt of the floor and prayed together. That was moving.

        2. For Minister of Defence - Laurie McMenemy. As you may know he's the manager of Southampton FC at the moment, but he's got the shoulders to shine on a wider stage than the green turf of Wembley. Southampton have played in Europe, so he's had invaluable experience of 'kicking the foreigners into the stands'. I assume he's a Tory, but I'm writing to him on your behalf to check. I certainly never saw a Socialist with a back as straight as his.

        3. For 'Our Man in Europe' - Paul Johnson. All right! All right! So they say he's a carrot-haired loony! So they call him Colonel 'Bonkers' Johnson! So what? Have they forgotten General Wolfe, the victor at Quebec? He was as mad as a hatter but he sent the Frogs packing! Johnson said to my father once:

        "Root! You and I are old enough to remember a time when you could walk from one end of the Champs Elysées to the other without seeing a Frenchman! Those were the days!"

        Johnson won't let you down, but watch out for the softies in the party. I don't much care for the look of Norman St John Stevas. My father taught me two things I've never forgotten.

        "Mind this, son," he used to say. "Never spit in a man's face unless his moustache is on fire. And never trust a man who wears mauve underpants at tea-time."

        I don't think we should have any bachelors in our Cabinet unless it's entirely necessary.

        Here's a pound!

        Bring back the rope! Let's go!

        Your man on the door-step!

        Henry Root.

Copies to: Mr Laurie McMenemy, Mr Paul Johnson and Mrs Whitehouse.

10 DOWNING STREET

10th May 1979

Dear Mr Root,

The Prime Minister has asked me to thank you very much for your letter of 4th May. Your message of congratulations is greatly appreciated and thank you very much for sending us another £1 for our Party funds.

With best wishes,

Yours Sincerely,

Richard Ryder

Richard Ryder
Political Office

Root Esq

SOUTHAMPTON FOOTBALL CLUB LIMITED Founded 1885

Registered office:
The Dell, Milton Road,
Southampton SO9 4XX

telephones:
(0703) 23408 & 28108

commercial office:
(0703) 38616

Manager
Lawrie McMenemy

Commercial Manager:
Malcolm Price

Secretary:
Brian Truscott

Dear Mr. Root,

LM/VG.

16th May, 1979.

Thank you for your considerations and I am very flattered that you put my name forward to Mrs. Thatcher. Should she decide to call on me perhaps you could let me know as soon as possible before I make too many plans for next season!

Seriously, I think she must have chosen her Cabinet by now and, like yourself, I do hope she does a good job.

Best wishes,

Yours sincerely,

Gardner

p.p. L. McMenemy,
Manager.   (Signed in his absence.)

Directors: A.A. Woodford (Chairman), John Corbett, B.G.W. Bowyer TD, JP,
Lt. Col. Sir George Meyrick Bart. MC, F.G.L. Askham FCA, E.T.Bates.

VAT Reg. No: 188 5098 14
Reg No: 53301 England

139 Elm Park Mansions
Park Walk
London, S.W.10.

D. Dudley Morgan Esq,
Theodore Goddard & Co,
16 St Martin-le-Grand,
London, E.C.1.   7th April 1979.

Dear Mr Morgan,

Your firm has been recommended to me as being one with some experience of the law. I address myself to you personally as the senior partner since I have litigation of some import to prosecute and I don't wish to find myself in the hands of the office-boy.

As the enclosed documents will show, I wrote to Mr Michael Edwardes of British Leyland on 31st March with the viable suggestion that the name of the company be changed to 'Japanese Leyland'.

As you will imagine, it was with a sense of outrage that I discovered on 4th April that my concept was already in the pipeline. By 5th April the matter had become public knowledge, as the enclosed cartoon will adequately demonstrate.

Mr Edwardes has not favoured me with the courtesy of a reply to my letter and I am now persuaded that he is of a mind to 'borrow' my notion without acknowledgement or payment.

You will agree that in the circumstances damages of unusual consequence would come my way in the High Court.

I look forward to hearing that you will act for me in this matter. I am in a position to put further work your way pursuant to a satisfactory assessment of your performance hereunder.

Yours faithfully,

Henry Root.

Henry Root.

THEODORE GODDARD & CO.

D. DUDLEY MORGAN
PETER A J MORLEY
J N FISHER
R DEREK FOX
BLANCHE H M A LUCAS
MARE N STACEY
MICHAEL Q WALTERS
F J CALDERAN
R K SHUTE
M J W TOD
EDWIN A JONES
WILLIAM S ROGERS
M A CROFT BAKER
M J HARRIS

ANTONY HEALD
CHRISTOPHER CLOGG
W H STUART MAY
ANDREW BINGHAM
MARTIN G CHESTER
P GRAFTON GREEN
DIANA GUY
DAVID S WILKINSON
R M PRESTON
DEREK W LEWIS
SIMON STUBBINGS
MARTIN KRANER
GUY I. F. LEIGH

R DEREK WISE C.B.E (RESIDENT IN PARIS)
EDWARD WILTSHIRE (RESIDENT IN MADRID)

CONSULTANT
DEREK F S CLOGG
ASSOCIATES

E. A. CLARKE
A R W CARRINGTON
C. J. J. MAPLES

DIANA SNEEZUM
NICHOLAS WHITNEY

16 ST. MARTIN'S-LE-GRAND
LONDON ECIA 4EJ

Telephone: 01-606 8855
Cables: Assumpsit London E.C.1
Telex: 884676
Telegrams: Assumpsit London Telex
Telecopier Extension 208
L.D.E. and C.D.E. Box Number 47
Stock Exchange Number STX 2346

Associate Offices:
167 RUE DE L'UNIVERSITE
PARIS 75007
Telephone (010 33) 705 89 45
Telex 25066I

LAGASCA 106
MADRID 6
Telephone (010 34 1) 275 03 24
Telegrams: Insertex

17 BOND STREET
ST HELIER, JERSEY C.I
Telephone (0534) 36576
Telex 41580

Your Ref

Our Ref   21

H. Root, Esq.,
139 Flm Park Mansions,
Park Walk,
London, S.W.10.

Dear Sir,

12th April, 1979.

Thank you for your letter of 7th April with enclosures concerning your possible complaint against Mr. Michael Edwards of British Leyland. I do not think I would necessarily agree with the penultimate paragraph of your letter that in the circumstances considerable damages would be awarded to you in the High Court.

In the circumstances this would not be a case which this firm would be prepared to undertake, and had we been prepared to do so we would have required very substantial sums on account before we accepted any instructions. If you still wish to proceed I suggest you seek some other firm who will be prepared to accept your instructions.

Yours faithfully,

D. DUDLEY MORGAN

139 Elm Park Mansions
Park Walk
London, S.W.10.

The Managing Director,
Hambros Bank Ltd,
41 Bishopsgate,
London, E.C.2.

9th May 1979.

Dear Sir,

For personal reasons which needn't concern you I am anxious
to acquire the book publishing house of Jonathan Cape Ltd.

You were not, in fact, my original choice to handle this
matter on my behalf. I first contacted the firm of Keyser
Ullman Ltd, but having read the so-called 'Selmes Report' I
decided to take my business elsewhere.

Not wishing to slip twice on the same banana skin, I had
my people run you through the computer. I have the print-out
on my desk now and I am glad to be able to tell you that you've
come up brand new. Well done! Indeed my people could find
nothing on you to suggest you're anything other than an honest
and diligent enterprise with no bad eggs under the table or
skeletons of an embarrassing nature in the cupboard.

In the circumstances I'd be happy for you to negotiate
the purchase of Jonathan Cape Ltd on my behalf. Perhaps you
could find out (without in the first instance divulging the
name of your client) the names of the present shareholders,
whether they could be 'induced' to sell, how many shares I
would have to buy to gain control and what the total cost to
myself would be.

I look forward to receiving your initial report and to
hearing what your own charges will be _if_ we're successful.

Yours faithfully,

Henry Root

Henry Root.

Hambros Bank Limited

Your ref

Out ref   CFD/ARB/MEB

41 Bishopsgate London EC2P 2AA
Telephone 01-588 2851 Telex 883851
Telegrams Hambro London EC2

11th May 1979

Henry Root, Esq.,
139 Elm Park Mansions,
Park Walk,
London, S.W.10.

Dear Sir,

Your letter of 9th May addressed to the Managing Director
has been passed to me. Jonathan Cape is a wholly owned subsidiary
of Chatto, Bodley Head & Jonathan Cape Ltd. and I would have thought
it unlikely that it would be for sale on its own.

However, if you want to discuss this matter further, please
do not hesitate to contact me.

Yours faithfully,

A.R. Beevor,
Director.

139 Elm Park Mansions
Park Walk
London, S.W.10.

Mr A.R. Beevor,   14th June 1979.
Hambros Bank Ltd,
41 Bishopsgate,
London, E.C.2.

Dear Beevor,

Please forgive me for not having been back to you sooner
with reference to my take-over of Jonathan Cape Ltd.

The fact is I've been flat to the boards here trying to
raise the wind to get the caper off the ground.

Don't hesitate to let me know if you have any sharp ideas
yourself in this direction! I could use them!

Stay cool. I'll be back to you soon.

Yours sincerely,

Henry Root.

Henry Root.

---

139 Elm Park Mansions
Park Walk
London, S.W.10.

Sir James Goldsmith,
Cavenham Foods,
Cavenham House,
Millington Road,
Hayes.

18th June 1979.

Dear Sir James,

I've been watching you for some time and you're all right!
If you decide to go into politics you can count on at least one
vote. Mine!

Your recent courageous stand against the cowardly bullies
in the media was just great!

If we stick together we can beat them. How much money do
they have? Not enough!

Here's a pound. Although you won your court case against
the weasel Gillard it's my experience that cowardly bullies don't
settle their bills as quickly as they promulgate a slander. The
pound's to help bridge the gap.

I believe you're presently showing a high profile in the
publishing racket. Well done! I'm about to go into publishing
myself with the purchase of the house of Cape. Do you know them?
All right once, not too sweet now. Perhaps we might get together
on this one. I'm looking for investors so if you're interested
why don't we grab a bite to eat some time?

What do you say we meet for lunch at your favourite watering-
hole, the Clermont Club, on Friday 29th June? I'd make it sooner,
but I'm flat to the boards with one thing and another at the moment.

I'm not a member of the Clermont myself, but no doubt you
can fix that. You get me in and I'll pay for lunch. How's that?
Fair enough?

I look forward to hearing from you and meeting on the 29th.
Freedom of speech except for blackmailers!

Yours sincerely,

Henry Root.

Henry Root.

Lord Chancellor's Department

Neville House Page Street London SW1P 4LS

Mr H Root,
139, Elm Park Mansions,
Park Walk,
LONDON SW10.   Date 9th May 1979

Dear Mr. Root,

I am writing on behalf of the Lord Chancellor to thank you for your letter of 28th March and apologise for the delay in replying.

I hope you will understand when I say from the outset that because our system of justice is based upon the independence of the courts from Government, it would be seen as a serious breach of this principle of judicial independence if the Lord Chancellor or any official of his department were to express views on the propriety of a sentence for any particular offence.

Parliament has given to all courts a complete discretion in the matter of sentencing subject in general to the maximum sentences which may be imposed for particular offences. The appropriate sentence for any circumstances of that case and the court, which has before it the full facts of the offence and usually the assistance of reports about the defendant's personal background and character, is in the best position to decide the correct way of dealing with him.

I do not know whether or not your attention was drawn to this case from newspaper reports, but if so, you will appreciate such reports must, of necessity, be brief and cannot possibly reflect all the conflicting factors that judges must consider when passing sentence.

It is not possible for me to be more helpful.

Yours sincerely

M A STEWART

139 Elm Park Mansions
Park Walk,
London, S.W.10.

Lord Hailsham,
The House of Lords,
London, S.W.1.   10th May 1979.

Dear Lord Hailsham,

   Well done! I wrote to your predecessor on 28th March
with a stiff complaint and what happened?

   Nothing!

   I then put the whole matter in your hands and what
happened?

   I got a reply by return of post!

   That's the Tory way! Keep it up!

   Support Mrs Thatcher!

Yours sincerely,

Henry Root.

139 Elm Park Mansions
Park Walk
London, S.W.10.

Curtis Brown Ltd,
1 Craven Hill,
London, W.2.   8th May 1979.

Dear Sir or Madam,

Please find enclosed a copy of my original play 'The English Way of Doing Things'.

It is a light-hearted romp in two acts about a Police Commissioner who sets forth in good shape to arrest the inmates of a bawdy-house but is flummoxed by the fact that they out-rank him socially. In a hilarious denouement he finds himself taking the bookings!

I would like to offer the part of the Police Commissioner to Sir Robert Mark.

As you will see, it's a small but telling part towards the end of the play, and I would venture to suggest exactly the sort of key but technically undemanding role that Sir Robert should be essaying at this stage of his acting career.

I think he could handle it, but we would of course require him to read for us.

I look forward to hearing from you.

Yours faithfully,

Henry Root.

Curtis Brown Limited

1 Craven Hill London W2 3EP

Henry Root, Esq.,
139 Elm Park Mansions,
Park Walk,
London, S.W.10.   11th May 1979

Dear Mr. Root,

Thank you very much for sending us THE ENGLISH
WAY OF DOING THINGS. I am sorry to say that Sir
Robert Mark is away in Australia for the next few
months and does not in any case feel that his talents lie
in the direction of acting.

I am therefore returning your script and I am sorry to
give you such a negative answer.

Yours sincerely,

Kate Marsh

139 Elm Park Mansions
Park Walk
London, S.W.10.

Head of Script Unit,
BBC Television Centre,
London, W.12.   9th May 1979.

Dear Sir,

Last night, Mrs Root and I were watching the excellent American TV (television) show 'McMillan & Wife', when I was struck by a sharp idea!

How about an English version of the show, called 'McNee & Wife', based of the crime-fighting exploits of our own Commissioner? Over the past few weeks I've been in close touch with Sir David McNee about his somewhat stodgy, not 'one 'o the People' image and I know he's keen to come across as less of a big Glasgow pudding to the general public. For this reason, I'm sure he'd cooperate if you came up with some good scripts based on his working day, showing him (like Rock Hudson) solving crimes and bringing wrong-doers to book with the able assistance of his lady wife and the family cook.

I happen to know he's very busy at the moment, so he might not have time to play the central role (though I could put it to him on your behalf.) It doesn't really matter, because I've had a *second* sharp idea! Now that he's an actor, who better to play the main character than Sir Robert Mark?

What do you say? I have a lot of clout with Sir Robert's agents, Curtis Brown, and I'll get straight on to them as soon as you give me the go-ahead.

[134]

As for the '& wife' character in the series, I doubt whether Lady Mark (not being a thespian like her husband) could handle it. Casting the part authentically should present no problems, however. Mrs Root is familiar with Lady Mark from afternoon bingo sessions in Esher and she tells me that either Hylda Baker or Thora Hird could portray her to the life. Whichever you preferred. Let's not butt heads over a minor character.

I look forward to receiving your go-ahead!

Yours sincerely,

Henry Root.

British Broadcasting Corporation

Television Centre Wood Lane London W12 7RJ

28th June, 1979

Dear Mr. Root,

I have received your letter of the 1st June and seen a copy of the letter to the Director General. As we receive 8,000 scripts a year which we deal with in strict rotation there is inevitably some delay in replying to authors. However, we have looked at your idea and I have to tell you that it is not remotely possible for television in this country for legal and copyright reasons not to mention the fact that it is our normal practice to only employ actors who are Equity members. Regarding copyright this is a very shady area and there is no strict copyright in ideas. For a brief outline of copyright law I refer you to the Writers' and Artists' Yearbook which should be available from your local public library.

Yours sincerely,

JOHN SCOTNEY
Head of Television Script Unit

139 Elm Park Mansions
Park Walk,
London, S.W.10.

The Managing Director,
Keyser Ullman Ltd,
25 Milk Street,
London, E.C.2.   3rd May 1979.

Dear Sir,

I wish to acquire the publishing house of Jonathan
Cape Ltd, of 30 Bedford Square, London, W.C.1.

You have been recommended to me as people who
can handle a delicate situation, so I'd be happy for you
to act for me in the matter.

Don't charge in like a bull at a gate. Use a little
stealth. I don't want Cape to see me coming, so in the
first instance just 'ask around' about the strength of the
present set-up. Who the present shareholders are,
whether we can 'get anything on them' etc etc. I don't
have to teach you your business.

We'll discuss your fees in the matter when you get in
touch with me with your initial report.

I look forward to hearing from you.

Yours faithfully,

Henry Root.

VERY URGENT

139 Elm Park Mansions
Park Walk
London, S.W.10.

The Managing Director,
Keyser Ullman Ltd,
25 Milk Street,
London, E.C.2.   8th May 1979.

Dear Sir,

Please ignore for the moment my letter of 3rd May with reference to my takeover of Jonathan Cape Ltd.

I have only just read the Department of Trade's so-called 'Selmes Report' and in the circumstances you will quite understand that I cannot allow you to proceed on my behalf until I have had you cleared.

I will be in touch with you with further instructions once I have checked out your present standing with the Department of Trade.

Do nothing until you hear from me again.

Yours faithfully,

Henry Root.

139 Elm Park Mansions
Park Walk
London, S.W.10.

The Managing Director,
Hambros Bank Ltd,
41 Bishopsgate,
London, E.C.2.   9th May 1979.

Dear Sir,

For personal reasons which needn't concern you I am anxious to acquire the book publishing house of Jonathan Cape Ltd.

You were not, in fact, my original choice to handle this matter on my behalf. I first contacted the firm Keyser Ullman Ltd, but having read the so-called 'Selmes Report' I decided to take my business elsewhere.

Not wishing to slip twice on the same banana skin, I had my people run you through the computer. I have the print-out on my desk now and I am glad to be able to tell you that you've come up brand new. Well done! Indeed my people could find nothing on you to suggest you're anything other than an honest and diligent enterprise with no bad eggs under the table or skeletons of an embarrassing nature in the cupboard.

In the circumstances I'd be happy for you to negotiate the purchase of Jonathan Cape Ltd on my behalf. Perhaps you could find out (without in the first instance divulging the name of your client) the names of the present shareholders, whether they could be 'induced' to sell, how many shares I would have to buy to gain control and what the total cost to myself would be.

I look forward to receiving your initial report and to hearing what your charges will be *if* we're successful.

Yours faithfully,

Henry Root.

Hambros Bank Limited

41 Bishopsgate London EC2P 2AA

Henry Root, Esq.,
139 Elm Park Mansions,
Park Walk,
London, S.W.10.   11th May 1979

Dear Sir,

   Your letter of 9th May addressed to the Managing
Director has been passed to me. Jonathan Cape is a
wholly owned subsidiary of Chatto, Bodley Head &
Jonathan Cape Ltd. and I would have thought it
unlikely that it would be for sale on its own.

   However, if you want to discuss this matter further,
please do not hesitate to contact me.

Yours faithfully.

A. R. Beevor,
Director.

139 Elm Park Mansions
Park Walk,
London, S.W.10.

The Department of Trade,
1 Victoria Street,
London, S.W.1.   25th May 1979.

Sir,

I seek your advice on a matter of considerable
urgency.

A week or two ago – before the publication of the
so-called 'Selmes Report' – I instructed the merchant
banking house of Keyser Ullman Ltd to purchase
Jonathan Cape Ltd, publishers of 30 Bedford Square,
London, W.C.1., on my behalf.

I was naturally most concerned when I read the
Selmes Report and now wonder whether I should leave
the matter in the hands of Keyser Ullman.

Could you let me know (confidentially, of course)
how Keyser Ullman shape up at the moment?

I cannot believe that Mr Edward du Cann – the man,
let it not be forgotten, who put Mrs Thatcher where she
is today – could have been associated with an
enterprise that reflected incompetence.

I look forward to hearing from you.

Yours faithfully,

Henry Root.

[142]

Department of Trade

Companies Division

2 – 14 Bunhill Row London EC1Y 8LL

Henry Root Esq
139 Elm Park Mansions
Park Walk
London
SW10.   Date 6 June 1979

Dear Mr Root

RE: FERGUSON & GENERAL INVESTMENTS LTD
(formerly known as Dowgate & General Investments
Ltd)
C S T INVESTMENTS LTD

Thank you for your letter of 25th May. I regret however,
that the Department is unable to advise you as to
whether or not, in the light of the Inspectors' Report, to
proceed with the purchase, through Keyser Ullmann
Ltd, of the Publishers, Jonathan Cape Ltd.

Yours sincerely

M B WOOLF

139 Elm Park Mansions
Park Walk
London, S.W.10.

The Managing Director,
Keyser Ullman Ltd,
25 Milk Street,
London, E.C.2.   12th June 1979

Dear Sir,

Please ignore *completely* my previous letters to you on the subject of my purchase of Jonathan Cape Ltd.

My man at the Department of Trade has now written to me as follows:

'I regret that the Department is unable to advise you as to whether or not, in the light of the Inspector's Report, to proceed with the purchase, through Keyser Ullman Ltd, of the publishers, Jonathan Cape Ltd'.

In the circumstances I have decided to instruct Hambros Ltd to act in this matter for me.

If you have already contacted (against my instructions) any of the principles involved in the matter, I must ask you to write to them immediately explaining that your company *is in no way* associated with Henry Root Wet Fish Ltd.

Yours faithfully,

Henry Root.

139 Elm Park Mansions
Park Walk
London, S.W.10.

Peter Barnes Esq,
The DPP's Office,
4 Queen Anne's Gate,
London, S.W.1.   11th May 1979.

Dear Mr Barnes,

Mrs Root and I were both flabbergasted by your
'performance' on 'TV Eye' last night.

I find it extraordinary that at a time when our Leader,
Mrs Thatcher, has appealed to the public to support the
police you, a public person, should see fit to go on
television to blackguard them.

No doubt your assessment, ringingly broadcast to the
country at large, that 95% of the Metropolitan CID are
as bent as a kangaroo's hind-leg is largely correct. Do
you really believe, however, that it is conducive to law
and order for the man in the street to be aware of this?
Could anything be better calculated to undermine the
thin blue line which stands between us and the
abolition of pay-beds than for the public at large to
know that the Met employs more criminals than it
catches?

I look forward to receiving an explanation, Sir, for
your extraordinary outburst.

Support Mrs Thatcher!

Yours sincerely,

Henry Root.

[145]

Department of Public Prosecutions

4–12 Queen Annes Gate London SW1H 9AZ

Henry Root Esq.
139 Elm Park Mansions
Park Walk
LONDON S.W.10.   Date   14th May 1979

Dear Mr. Root,

   I answer to your letter of 11th May, I can assure you
that in the T.V. Eye programme I neither said nor
implied that 95% of the Metropolitan CID are corrupt.

   Indeed my personal view is that the percentage of
corrupt policeman is very small although, as I did point
out in the interview, it is very hard to get sufficient
evidence to ensure the conviction of those few.

   The overwhelming majority of the police do a
magnificent job and they fully deserve the support and
confidence of the public.

   Yours sincerely,

   P. R. BARNES

139 Elm Park Mansions
Park Walk
London, S.W.10.

The Rt Hon William Whitelaw,
The Home Office,
Whitehall,
London, S.W.1.   18th May 1979.

Dear Mr Whitelaw,

   Well done! You gave me your assurance in your letter
of 2nd April that when you came to power you
'intended to build up the strength and quality of the
police to give them a better opportunity to investigate
and prevent crime'. Already you have raised their pay!
Congratulations! Soon the 'thin blue line' will become
the 'thick blue line'! How splendid to have a
Government which fulfils the promises in its manifesto!

   However. In your letter to me of 27th April you
wrote:

   'I can confirm that our Conservative Party will take
action against pornography'.

   Excellent. But what bothers me is this. I read recently
that 60% of all drugs on the black-market had been put
there by the police. No sooner are drugs seized, it
seems, than they are recycled onto the street by the
arresting officers!

   Can you assure me that the same thing won't happen
with pornography? It would be a scandal, in my
opinion, if all the material confiscated from family
bookshops turned up a few weeks later, and, as is the
case with drugs apparently, at a grossly inflated price,

due to the Porn Squad's profit margin having to be tacked on the top.

I know our Leader, Mrs Thatcher, is in favour of private enterprise, but this is the free market gone mad! I don't want to see the price of 'Rendezvous' going through the roof just because some ambitious Detective Inspector (spurred on, no doubt, by Mrs Thatcher's exhortations that he should stand on his own two feet) is buying a new split-level maisonette with lounge-diner in Godolming.

One would have somewhat greater faith in the average policeman's awareness of what constitutes an acceptable profit had not Mr Peter Barnes of the DPP's office gone on television last week to announce in 'TV Eye' that in his opinion most of the Metropolitan CID were as bent as corkscrews.

Yours for the Market Economy Within Reasonable Limits!

Henry Root.

139 Elm Park Mansions
Park Walk,
London, S.W.10.

Kenneth Rose Esq,
The Sunday Telegraph,
Fleet Street,
London, E.C.4.   14th May 1979.

Dear Mr Rose,

Your gossip column in 'The Sunday Telegraph' is
often lively. Well done! But yesterday you had an item
perplexing to the self-made man such as myself who
has taken well to the paper after a poor start.

Writing of Mr Gordon Richardson, the Governor of
the Bank of England (nice job!), you call him a man of
'civilised tastes'.

What are these? For my sort you must spell things
out. With Mrs Thatcher pouring the sherry wine it will
be even more important, if one wants to hold on in the
lounge-rooms of power, to know what civilised tastes
are.

Don't misunderstand me, Kenneth. I don't walk
around with a straw up my nose and my trousers held
at the knee with harvesting twine. I know, for instance,
that one shouldn't ask one's hostess for directions to the
'toilet', listen to Shirley Bassey records or tell German
jokes in the presence of the Royal Family. But Mr
Richardson must know more about 'civilised tastes'
than this, otherwise I'd be Governor of the Bank of
England. Right?

I'd appreciate some guidelines in this area and to this

end I enclose three colour snaps of myself and Mrs Root taken at the Derby last year.

I want you to come straight out and tell us whether we shape up. Don't pull your punches. If you think Mrs Root looks like an old belter, you say so. Bear in mind, however, that following a bit of luck on the 4.30 she's being escorted off the course by a constable prior to being booked on a D & D infringement. Even Mr Richardson wouldn't be at his best in such a corner, I think you'll agree.

And how about me? I might say that my suit and topper are not on hire by the hour from Covent Garden or bought with coupons. No sir. They put me back a couple of hundred quid.

Perhaps I should say that I'm 45, that I've made a fortune in wet fish and, since I've sold my business and retired, that I've got time on my hands in which to devote myself to the study of 'civilised tastes'.

Let's hear from you!

Cheers!

Henry Root.

As from

Sunday Telegraph

138 Fleet Street London EC4P 4BL

May 15, 1979

Dear Mr. Root,

Thank you for your letter of May 14, which I interrupt a holiday to answer.

By Gordon Richardson's 'civilised tastes' (in the context of his possible appointment as head of an Oxford college) I meant that he is well-read with an impressive knowledge of pictures and music.

I write a weekly column and do not run correspondence courses on etiquette: so I should regard it as very impertinent on my part to suggest how others should behave in matters of speech or recreation.

All I would say of the photographs you send me (and which I now return) is that you seem to be having more fun than most people at the Derby. Did you back a winner?

Glad to hear you made a fortune out of fish. That, I suppose, is why I can no longer afford it!

All good wishes,

Yours sincerely,

Kenneth Rose

139 Elm Park Mansions
Park Walk
London, S.W.10.

H.R.H. The Prince of Wales,
c/o Buckingham Palace, (please forward)
London, S.W.1.
18th May 1979.

Your Royal Highness,

Inspired by the example of your uncle, Lord Mountbatten, I have decided to throw my flat open to the public on Saturday 9th June.

I reckon to pull in the Japs and the more gullible of our American friends. The idea is to show them how an *ordinary* English couple lives.

I'll take the mugs on a conducted tour of the premises while Mrs Root and my two youngsters, Doreen (19) and Henry Jr (15), continue doing what any average family does at weekends: that is to say stretching the family budget by bottling plums, lolling about painting one's finger-nails and carrying out the weekly bullworker maintenance. Mrs Root will be bottling plums, Doreen will be oiling her bullworker and Henry Jr will be painting his finger-nails, but that's young people these days.

Would you consider performing the opening ceremony? We'd be very honoured and it would be nice for you to meet my Doreen. If you found yourself a little short, I'd be prepared, like your uncle Lord

Mountbatten, to sock you the pound entrance fee till you straightened up.

I look forward to hearing from you, Sir.

Support Mrs Thatcher!

Yours respectfully,

Henry Root. A naval man like yourself!

P.S. Sorry to send this care of Her Majesty, but you don't seem to be in the phone book.

BUCKINGHAM PALACE

From: The Assistant Private Secretary to H.R.H. The Prince of Wales

4th June, 1979.

Dear Mr Root,

   The Prince of Wales has asked me to thank you very much for your letter to him of 18th May in which you asked if he would be able to visit your flat on Saturday 9th June.
   I am afraid His Royal Highness will be unable to accept your kind invitation since he has already made his plans for that day.

Yours sincerely,

Oliver Everett

Henry Root, Esq.

139 Elm Park Mansions
Park Walk
London, S.W.10.

H.E. The Greek Ambassador,
The Greek Embassy,
1a Holland Park,
London, W.11.   30th April 1979.

Your Excellency,

   I write to you on a matter which could have serious
international repercussions.

   Yesterday afternoon Mrs Root was hosing down the
family Rolls under my supervision when her knees
gave forth, causing her to sit in the bucket and rick her
back. A massage appeared to be the answer, so we
summoned a young lady whose advertisement in the
window of our local newsagent proclaimed 'Greek
Masseuse. Full Theatrical Wardrobe'. (Mrs Root
naturally didn't want some fancy man offering to oblige
her separately.)

   All was proceeding according to the book, when
Arianna – for that was the young lady's name –
suddenly sat athwart Mrs Root and suggested sapphic
alternatives with the door closed.

   Sir, is this the Greek way of doing things? Is this some
indigenous custom of your once great country,
instigated by such celebrated homosexualists as Plato
the Great and General Alexander and kept alive by such
as the big warbling pudding who crops up from time to
time on 'Top of the Pops'?

   Mrs Root screeched like a gibbon and Arianna high-
tailed it out of the flat with her bag of tricks, but Mrs

[155]

Root was so shaken by the incident that I had to get my own dinner. In the circumstances we have thought it best to cancel a sunshine holiday for two we had planned to take this summer in your part of the world, where no doubt swimming without clothes and the eating of raw fish is now encouraged.

I would suggest, Mr Ambassador, that you take immediate action to dissuade those of Miss Arianna's stripe from bringing the rest of you into disrepute.

Such incidents as the one I have described could never have happened under the Colonels.

Yours respectfully,

Henry Root.

Copy to The Foreign Office.

139 Elm Park Mansions
Park Walk
London, S.W.10.

The Greek Ambassador,
1a Holland Park,
London, W.11.   1st June 1979.

Your Excellency,

   I am astonished that you haven't had the common
civility to reply to my letter of 30th April re Mrs Root's
experience at the hands of one of your masseuses.

   What's going on over there in Holland Park? Get a
grip on yourself, my good man!

   I look forward to hearing from you by return.

Yours sincerely,

Henry Root.

Copy to Sir Ian Gilmour, The Foreign Office.

Consulate General of Greece

1A Holland Park, London W11 3TP

Henry Root, Esq.,
139 Elm Park Mansions,
Park Walk,
LONDON S.W.10.   7th June, 1979.

Dear Sir,

   We acknowledge receipt of your letters dated 30th
April and 1st June addressed to His Excellency the
Ambassador and which have been forwarded to me.

   I am sorry for the trouble which has been caused to
your wife but, as you will understand, it is not a matter
of the competence of this Consulate General and I
suggest that if you wish to pursue the matter you
should contact the competent British authorities.

Yours faithfully,
For Consul General

P. Vlassopoulos
Consul

Foreign and Commonwealth Office

London SW1A 2AH

Henry Root Esq
139 Elm Park Mansions
Park Walk
LONDON SW10   Date 6 June 1979

Dear Mr Root

I have been asked to thank you for your letter of 1 June
to Sir Ian Gilmour, the contents of which have been
noted. The incident you describe is indeed regrettable. I
hope that Mrs Root's back is better.

Yours sincerely

A L S Coltman
Southern European Department

139 Elm Park Mansions
Park Walk
London, S.W.10.

Mr A.L.S. Coltman,
Southern European Department,
The Foreign and Commonwealth Office,
London, S.W.1.   21st June 1979.

Dear Mr Coltman,

Thank you for your letter of 6th June re the incident of Mrs Root and the Greek 'masseuse'.

She's on the mend now, you'll be relieved to hear, though she still gets the jitters from time to time, being unable to watch without qualms Miss Esther Rantzen on TV or confront a portion of moussaka.

Please thank Sir Ian Gilmour for taking an interest in this matter. Don't bother Lord Carrington with it. I'm sure he's got enough to worry about what with one thing and another here and there.

Perhaps I could seek your advice on another matter while I have your attention. Having cancelled our annual holiday for two in Greece consequent upon Mrs Root's 'experience', we are now wondering whether the sunshine island of Ibiza might make a viable alternative. Once was when the holder of a British passport could move through Europe and other parts knowing that his person and the persons of his family were adequately protected by the signature of Her Majesty's Foreign Secretary on page 1. Not anymore, it seems. I have heard rumours that even in Spain matters are not, since the sad death of General Franco, all that they might be re law and order. As so often happens, democracy, it seems, has brought in its wake swarms of local Pedros who roam the streets putting their hands up ladies' skirts and infiltrating to their own ends the wallet-pockets of package tourists.

Can you, Sir, as a Southern European expert, tell me whether these practices have now reached the Balearics or whether in fact Mrs Root and I could safely visit Ibiza this summer without incident?

Yours sincerely,

Henry Root.

Foreign and Commonwealth Office

London SW1A 2AH

Henry Root Esq
139 Elm Park Mansions
Park Walk
London SW10

Date 27 June 1979

Dear Mr Root

Thank you for your letter of 21 June. I am glad that Mrs Root is better.

I know no reason why you should not visit Ibiza. But the activities to which you refer are indeed apt to occur in most popular tourist centres. A travel agent should be able to advise on this aspect.

Yours sincerely

A L S Coltman
Southern European Department

139 Elm Park Mansions
Park Walk
London, S.W.10.

C. James Anderton Q.P.M., F.B.I.M.,
Chief Constable's Office,
Chester House,
Boyer Street,
Manchester M16 0RE.   21st May 1979.

Dear Chief Constable,

May I congratulate you on your fine showing on the
TV programme 'Jaywalking' yesterday evening?

You came over as forceful and sincere – in marked
contrast, may I say, to our own Sir David McNee, who
recently made a very poor fist of being interviewed on
'Thames at 6'. He shaped up well physically, but under
Andrew Gardner's relentless probing his brain fell out
and he admitted, among other things, that half his force
was corrupt! Not very good for the morale of those
under him! You'd never fall into such an obvious trap!

One slight criticism. Questioning you about your
sensible decision to give full police protection (at a cost
of hundreds of thousands of pounds to the rate-payers)
to a recent National Front rally on your patch (as you so
rightly understand, freedom of speech – however
obnoxious – *must* be protected by the law, though this
freedom must *never* be extended to pornographers),
Miss Jay said:

"Was that a moral decision or a police decision?"

My eldest, Doreen, who is reading philosophy and
sociology at Essex University, said that either this was a

[163]

category mistake (whatever that might be!) or Miss Jay was implying that a police decision can never be a moral decision.

If my Doreen is correct (and it wouldn't be the first time, I might add), may I ask you why you didn't thrust Miss Jay's question back down her throat by saying something along the lines of:

"Are you suggesting, madam, that there must always be a clear distinction between a moral decision and a police decision? I recognise no such distinction."

Apart from this one slight lapse – a really splendid performance! Well done!

Keep it up!

Christians demand the return of the rope!

Your pal in the soft south!

Henry Root.

C James Anderton, Q.P.M., F.B.I.M.

Chief Constable

Chief Constable's Office
P.O. Box 22 (S. West PDO)
Chester House
Boyer Street
Manchester M16 0RE

22nd May 1979.

Dear Mr. Root,

It was kind of you to write to me on 21st May and I
appreciate your good wishes.

Your daughter Doreen is absolutely right in her
opinion of my handling of the question to which you
specifically refer. The trouble is that, in a lengthy
television interview during which questions come thick
and fast, it is not possible always to sort out one's
thoughts quickly enough to meet the situation
correctly. In any event, the whole thing was
pre-recorded and later chopped about in such a way
that one cannot guarantee that the questions and
answers are put together properly. You will know
television interviewers often film their own questions
later to complete the programme.

If I had dealt with the question better to meet the point raised by your daughter, I am quite sure it would not have featured in the programme at all.

Thank you for your interest.

Yours sincerely,

Chief Constable.

Henry Root, Esq.,
139 Elm Park Mansions,
Park Walk,
London, S.W.10.

139 Elm Park Mansions
Park Walk
London, S.W.10.

The Producer,
'Brass Tacks',
BBC,
Manchester.   23rd May 1979.

Dear Sir,

I wish to protest most strongly at the scandalous treatment this country's finest policeman, Mr James Anderton, received on your programme last night.

To sit a fine Christian gentleman down in close proximity to an unsavoury crowd of prostitutes was bad enough. Even worse was to allow him to be humiliated intellectually by the afore-mentioned rabble (when you must have known perfectly well that it is not given to mere policemen, as it is to street-walkers, to think coherently on their feet.) Worst of all was your irresponsible decision not to cut out the ringingly audible aside made by one of the ladies of the night, who suddenly turned to the painted strumpet sitting on her left and said, in a whisper which must have echoed round the country:

"This sanctimonious, dirty-minded half-wit really gets on my tits! I hate to think how *he* gets his rocks off!"

Your programme, apart from being an aid and comfort to every prostitute in the land, Sir, must have put the cause of Law and Order back by fifty years.

I await your explanation.

Yours disgusted,

Henry Root.

P.S. I would be grateful if you could supply me with the phone number of the young lady with red hair who sat in the centre and did most of the talking. I would like to contact her with reference to my own researches.

British Broadcasting Corporation

New Broadcasting House Box 27 Oxford Road
Manchester M60 1SJ

Mr. Henry Root,
139, Elm Park Mansions,
Park Walk,
London, S.W.10.   20th June, 1979.

Dear Mr. Root,

In the absence of our Editor, Roger Laughton, your
letter has been passed to me by the Programme
Controller's office for reply.

As you know, at the end of BRASS TACKS we advertise
a service to viewers who wish to express a point of view
on the subject under discussion. That's in a programme
called RETURN CALL transmitted on the Monday
following the programme. In fact, an excerpt from your
letter was used in that programme on 28th May 1979.

> "Your programme, apart from being an aid and
> comfort to every prostitute in the land, Sir, must have
> put the cause of Law and Order back fifty years."

As you will realise the response to such a subject was
overwhelming and we received several hundred
letters, which makes it quite impossible to furnish
individual replies to all of them. May I say that of all the
people who have written with a point of view on the
subjects we have covered, this is the first time that
anyone has objected to not getting a personal reply.

To take up some of the other points in your first letter, a
copy of which we retain on our files, I have reviewed

[169]

the tape of the original transmission and can at no point hear anyone saying:

> "This sanctimonious, dirty-minded half-wit really gets on my tits! I hate to think how *he* gets his rocks off!"

Finally, I am afraid it is not our policy to release the telephone numbers of programme guests. However, if you wish, I am quite happy to forward a letter from you to the young lady in question and then leave it to her discretion as to whether or not she chooses to reply.

Yours sincerely,

Eric Robson,
Presenter,
BRASS TACKS.

139 Elm Park Mansions
Park Walk
London, S.W.10.

Mr Eldon Griffiths MP,
The House of Commons,
London, S.W.1.   26th May 1979.

Dear Eldon,

I was delighted to read in the paper this week that
you are already planning to raise the 'restoration of
hanging' issue in the House. Well done! Once again
ordinary folk have a Government which cares a little
for their safety.

I have a suggestion to make, on which I'd appreciate
your comments. One of the arguments for capital
punishment rests on the deterrent value of the rope.
Couldn't it be argued that hanging is too swift a
method of execution to deter the really hard-line
criminal?

I expect you were as impressed as I was to read of the
recent execution in Florida of a character called John
Spenkelink in the electric chair. It seems a full six
minutes passed before Spenkelink was dead, during
which time he hopped about like a prawn on a hot-
plate.

That will have taught him to think twice in future
before shooting innocent people.

Wouldn't the prospect of being slowly fried to a crisp
be more alarming to the terrorists and sex fiends who
are making it impossible for decent folk to walk our

streets than the mere prospect of dangling at the end of a rope?

Let me have your views on this.

Support Mrs Thatcher!

Yours for the introduction of the chair!

Henry Root.

.... Alan Swfkllton M P ....

acknowledges with thanks the receipt of your communication

of the .... 26th May ....

the contents of which have been noted.

8/77 12m 335617 LP1-2029   H.C. 85

[173]

139 Elm Park Mansions
Park Walk
London, S.W.10.

Mr George Hardy,
Derby County Football Club,
The Baseball Ground,
Derby.   28th May 1979.

Dear George,

I'm a busy man, but you're in a deep hole with the
Rams and I'm prepared to dig you out. I'm hereby
nominating myself for the job of manager, as
advertised.

Right. Down to cases. You'll want to know what
experience I've had of running a football club.

None at all!

So what? The name of the game is motivation and
psychology, and *that* I know about. Why do you
suppose Mr Clough consistently delivered the
goods? Because he terrorises the lads into turning it
on for him, that's why. I'll be the same. I'll have the
lads so psyched up they'll run round the park like
demented threshing-machines, reducing even
Liverpool's Red Army to a bunch of dancing
woofters.

In one respect only will I carry on with policies of
my predecessor, the Doc. I'll get rid of all the good
players. (He only left two behind – Daly and the boy
Hill – so this won't take long.) Psychology again, you
see. The players who stay behind will feel less bad
about their uselessness out there on the park.

I gather you've got a few bad eggs under the board-room table. They'll have to go. Leave this to me.

It so happens that I'll be in Derby on business on Tuesday 12th June. If I don't hear from you to the contrary, I'll assume it will be okay for me to drop in and see you at the Baseball Ground at about 12.30. We can finalise the details – salary, perks, kick-backs etc – then.

Let me know if you can't make it. I'd be as sick as a parrot to run into your office only to discover that you were visiting your 'masseuse'.

Up the Rams!

It's all about winning!

Yours,

Henry Root.

Derby County Football Club Limited

The Baseball Ground
Derby DE3 8NB

12th July 1979

Dear Sir

We thank you for your letter applying for the position of Manager with our Club.

We regret to inform you that your application was unsuccessful, the Club having appointed Mr. Colin Addison to the position.

May we thank you for your interest and we wish you every success in the future.

Yours faithfully

George Hardy
Chairman

139 Elm Park Mansions
Park Walk
London, S.W. 10.

Nicholas Scott MP,
The House of Commons,
London, S.W. 1.   28th May 1979.

Dear Mr Scott,

During the recent election campaign you were good
enough to answer my questions most promptly.

In the event, I'm afraid I was unable to vote for you
(as you will remember, we were unable to resolve our
differences over the selective hanging issue) but you
are, for better or worse, my MP, so I wonder if I might
trouble you again.

Following the adverse publicity given to the
behaviour of the Scottish football fans on Saturday last,
the false and misleading comparisons between the
dangers of alcohol and so-called cannabis are once
again being made. The 'legalise cannabis' lobby in the
media has been quick to draw our attention to the
violence, blood-shed and damage to property caused
by the high-spirited Tartan Army, and equally quick to
point out that far from inducing this kind of anti-social
behaviour cannabis, in fact, has a strangely peaceable
and law-abiding effect on those who take it.

So what? A drop of the hard stuff never hurt anyone.
Most parents, as I'm sure you will agree, would
infinitely prefer that their youngsters were exposed to a
bit of boisterous horse-play by a few thousand bottle-
throwing football fans than that they should 'drop out'
of reality by taking cannabis.

[177]

Can I have your assurance that you will never vote for any bill designed to legalise cannabis or one to restrict the easy distribution of alcohol?

Support Mrs Thatcher!

Yours for a wee drop!

Henry Root.

Nicholas Scott, MBE, MP

7 June 1979

Dear Mr Root

Thank you for your letter.

'Never' is an extravagant word in the
political lexicon, but I do fully share
your views about the dangers of legalising
cannabis and I have little fear that I shall
become hooked on the evidence of counter-
vailing opinion.

As for alochol, I must admit it would
be against my natural inclinations and
better judgement to seek to control its
consumption.

Yours sin——

Henry Root Esq.

Nicholas Scott

Mr 'Larry' Lamb,
The Sun,
30 Bouverie Street,
London, E.C.4.   25th May 1979.

Dear Mr Lamb,

I wish to protest most strongly about a story which appears on the front page of 'The Sun' today.

Under a picture of a foreign 'actress' (no doubt French) called Suzanne Danielle, we are informed that she lives with a Mr Patrick Mower in a Buckinghamshire cottage.

I don't want to know that! Nor, I may say, does Mrs Root.

Is it due to some sub-clause in the Treaty of Rome that we now have to be brought up to date over our breakfast cornflakes with the immoral arrangements of foreign 'actresses' living in this country? Such information should be tucked away on page 3, if anywhere.

Why can't you publish on your front page a picture of the gracious and talented English actress, Miss Nanette Newman, with the information that *she is living with her husband*, the equally talented Mr Bryan Forbes, in a villa in Virginia Water?

I look forward to receiving your explanation, Sir, for this thinly veiled attack on family values.

Support Mrs Thatcher!

Yours sincerely,

Henry Root.

Copy to Sir David Nicholson (56, married, 3 grown-up children – Euro candidate.)

139 Elm Park Mansions
Park Walk
London, S.W.10.

Sir David Nicholson,
10 Fordie House,
Sloane Street,
London, S.W.1.   25th May 1979.

Dear Sir David,

I enclose a copy of a letter I have today written to Mr
'Larry' Lamb of Sun Newspapers Ltd.

Before I cast my vote for you in the coming European
election, could you let me know where you stand on
this sort of issue?

In my view the Common Market should be about
morality as well as butter mountains. What do you
think?

I see from your leaflet that you speak fluent French
and have a knowledge of Germans. Do you know
something we don't?

Support Mrs Thatcher!

Yours sincerely,

Henry Root. Anti-Marketeer.

THE SUN
News Group Newspapers Ltd
30 Bouverie Street, Fleet Street, London, EC4Y 8DE.

Henry Root, Esq.,
139 Elm Park Mansions,
Park Walk,
London, SW10.   May 30th, 1979.

Dear Mr Root

Thank you for your letter.

I understand – without necessarily accepting – your point of view.

We are in the business of supplying information. Doctor Who is a very popular programme. Mr. Mower is a very popular actor.

To record the fact of his domestic arrangement with Ms. Danielle surely does not imply approval of the arrangement.

My apologies to Mrs. Root!

With best wishes,

Yours sincerely,

Larry Lamb,
EDITOR

DAVID NICOLSON
Conservative Candidate

Central Committee Room: 90 Ebury St. SW1W 9QD

Henry Root, Esq.,
139, Elm Park Mansions,
Park Walk,
LONDON S.W.10.   30th May, 1979.

Dear Mr Root,

Many thanks for your letter of May 25th, and I can
only say that I too deplore the kind of article to which
you refer and which appears so often in the popular
press.

I believe if we had a proper national objective once
again and concentrated on other things, we could
certainly improve standards of morality.

Yours sincerely,

David Nicolson

139 Elm Park Mansions
Park Walk
London, S.W.10.

The Chairman,
The Parole Board,
50 Queen Anne's Gate,
London, S.W.1.   30th May 1979.

Dear Sir,

   May I, a mere member of the general public, congratulate you on your enlightened decision to release ex-Commander Kenneth Drury, late of the Flying Squad?

   In my opinion a policeman should never be sent to prison, no matter what he's done. It's outrageous that he should be obliged to mingle with common criminals, many of whom he will have been obliged to 'fit up' in the execution of his duty.

   Perhaps I could take this opportunity of suggesting parole for the so-called Luton Post Office killers. Not because they happen to be innocent. In the interests of law and order that's neither here nor there. No, I suggest clemency merely on the grounds that their sentence seemed a little harsh. Ten years is about right for something you didn't do; twenty is definitely too long.

   I look forward to hearing your views on this suggestion.

Yours faithfully,

Henry Root.

Copy to Mr Timothy Raison MP.

PAROLE BOARD

Queen Anne's Gate
London, SW1H 9AT

Mr H Root
139 Elm Park Mansions
Park Walk
LONDON
SW10

17th July 1979

Dear Mr Root

Thank you for your letter of 30 May to which the
Chairman of the Parole Board has asked me to reply on
his behalf. The delay in replying is regretted.

I should perhaps explain that the Parole Board is an
independent non-judicial advisory body only and can
only consider and recommend on cases which have
been referred to it by the Home Secretary. This applies
equally to prisoners with determinate sentences or with
life sentences, and until the Home Secretary sees fit to
refer the cases you mention to it, the Parole Board has
no authority to comment on the matter of their parole
suitability.

I should also add that the question of a prisoner's guilt
or innocence is not a matter for the Parole Board. The
Board can only proceed on the premise that parole
candidates are guilty of the crimes they have been
convicted of by the Courts and sentenced accordingly.

I have copied this correspondence to the Home Office
for their information.

Yours sincerely

Home Office

Queen Anne's Gate London SW1H 9AT

H Root Esq
139 Elm Park Mansions
Park Walk
LONDON
SW10   Date   27 July 1979

Dear Sir

You wrote to Mr Raison on 1 June asking for his comments on a copy of a letter which you had sent to the Chairman of the Parole Board.

On the first point (that police officers convicted of offences should not be sent to prison) the sentence to be imposed in a particular case is, within the limits provided by the law and subject to the right of appeal, for the Court to decide in the light of all the information before it about the offence and the offender. It would be wholly inappropriate for the Home Secretary, or any Government Minister for that matter, to attempt to interfere with the Court's discretion in an individual case.

On the second point (that those convicted of the murder of the Luton sub-postmaster should now be released on parole) prisoners serving life sentences are not eligible for parole as such but are released on a life licence under the terms of which they may be recalled to prison at any time during the remainder of their lives should their conduct make this necessary. But the Home Secretary cannot order the release of a life sentence prisoner unless he is recommended to do so by the Parole Board and after he has consulted the Lord Chief Justice and, if he is available, the trial judge. Each case is dealt with

[187]

individually on its own merits and, in considering the case of any life sentence prisoner, the Parole Board and the Home Secretary must proceed on the basis that the prisoner was rightly convicted. The cases of those convicted of the murder of the Luton sub-postmaster will be considered in precisely the same way as those of all other prisoners serving life sentences for murder.

Yours faithfully

MRS V K STOREY

Root House
139 Elm Park Mansions
Park Walk
London, S.W.10.

Lord Grade,
ACC Ltd,
ATV House,
London, W.1.

1st June 1979.

Dear Lord Grade,

I'm presently getting together a consortium of plausible businessmen to take over the publishing house of Jonathan Cape.

I don't know whether you're familiar with this company. It once enjoyed a solid reputation in the world of letters, but recently, due to lack of editorial know-how and ability to pick winning manuscripts with lucrative subsidiary rights situations attached, it has gone back badly.

It is my opinion, however, that with the right go-go management (me) directing its affairs, in place of the grey-beards and dizzy young girls now in control, it could once again have a relevant contribution to make to the literary scene.

Would you be interested in joining the consortium? My bankers, Hambros, are pressing me for a meeting, but first I want to arrange some financial back-up. Under-capitalised, I'd be running through Hambros' door in nothing but my bowler hat and that would create a doubtful impression.

You appeal to me as a man who can make up his mind

quickly (well done!) so if the concept strikes you as valid perhaps you'd like to have lunch (on me!) at the Mirabelle at 1 o'clock on Friday 15th June.

May I say how much I'm looking forward to your Euro-Gala from the Theatre Royal, Drury Lane this Sunday? Miss Petunia Clark is a splendid artiste and melodies to catch the ear always appeal to the family.

You're a true European!

I look forward to hearing from you.

Yours for family entertainment!

Henry Root.

Associated Communications Corporations Limited

ATV House 17 Great Cumberland Place London W1A 1AG

H. Root, Esq.,
139 Elm Park Mansions,
Park Walk,
London, SW.10.   6th June, 1979

Dear Mr. Root,

   Lord Grade has passed to me your letter of the 1st June concerning your proposition to buy the book publishing house of Jonathan Cape Limited. We actually looked at this particular company some twelve months ago and decided not to attempt to purchase it.

   We hope that you will be successful in obtaining someone else to join your consortium.

Yours sincerely,

Jack Gill.

139 Elm Park Mansions,
Park Walk,
London, S.W.10.

Miss Debra Byron,
Editorial,
Jonathan Cape Ltd,
30 Bedford Square,
London, W.C.1.

2nd June 1979.

Dear Miss Byron,

Thank you for your letter of 20th April with regard to my original novel, 'Day of Reckoning'. I must apologise for not getting back to you before now.

You'll be delighted to know that your prompt and courteous rejection of the book as it then stood in no way drove me from my typewriter! Rather the reverse! This, I suspect, was your intention. As you quickly perceived, you weren't dealing with silly young girl with her head filled with maudlin literary dreams of an Irish saint, but with a plain-speaking man with whom you needn't pull your editorial punches.

I know one can't expect instant success. After all, isn't it the case that Freddy Forsyth's 'The Day of the Jackass' was turned down with ill-concealed contempt by no less than 37 of the top houses including your own (well done!)

So did I give up? No sir! I had a long hard look at the piece (particularly the ending – so often the weakest part of a first book) and came to the conclusion that there might be something valid in what you said.

So I went to work! Here, after six hard weeks are the fruits of your editorial know-how and my perseverence. What I have done, as you will quickly see, is tighten up the prose and cut ruthlessly (without, I hope, destroying the book's artistic integrity) so we are left with nothing but the hard muscle of the narrative line. Now the reader is led unerringly by the nose to the book's psychological centre – our hero's actual moment of reckoning, the moment when he discovers who he really is.

Other deft touches have been to alter the main character's name to Harry Toro (this renders the work less distractingly autobiographical) and to change the name of a subsiduary character from Lorraine Pumptit (weak) to Desirée Thunderbottom (much stronger).

Okay, the ball's back in your court! Let's go!

Yours sincerely,

Henry Root.

DAY OF RECKONING

by

HENRY ROOT

2nd Draft

Amazingly attractive, 45-year-old Harry Toro, chairman of Harry Toro Wet Fish Ltd woke up in the bedroom of his luxury mansion in Maidenhead.

He began to count his blessings. His Rolls, his swimming-pool, the expense account trips to Paris and New York with his latest 'companion', the long-legged, full-bosomed 'starlet', Desiree Thunderbottom.

Suddenly he felt guilty. He thought of the back-streets of Barnsley in which he'd been born and in which his aged parents still lived. Were he to get up now, take the Rolls from the garage and and drive himself, literally and metaphorically, back to his origins would he still have anything to say to his old mum and dad, to his mates at the local factory and to little Janet Gibbens with whom he'd had his first 'experience' at the local Odeon?

"Who cares?" he thought, and he went happily back to sleep.

THE END

Henry Root
139 Elm Park Mansions
Park Walk
London, S.W.7.

ALL RIGHTS RESERVED

Jonathan Cape Limited

Thirty Bedford Square
London W.C.1.

Mr Henry Root,
139 Elm Park Mansions,
Park Walk,
London, S.W.10.   6th June, 1979

Dear Mr Root,

Thank you for your letter of 2nd June and a copy of your synopsis for DAY OF RECKONING. We regret that we still do not think it would be worth your while submitting your novel to us and we wish you success in placing it with another publisher.

Yours sincerely,

Debra Byron,
Editorial.

End: Synopsis

139 Elm Park Mansions
Park Walk
London, S.W.10.

Petal Model Agency Ltd,
28 Walpole Street,
London, S.W.3.   6th June 1979.
                                 (D-Day plus 35 years!)

Dear Sir or Madame,

In case you are unfamiliar with my work, let me say at once that I am a photographer not without experience and flair, known for the standard of my finish here and there. Also fully equipped with Hasselblad and strobe.

You have been given to me as the people to supply the best type of girl for outdoor photography without clothes.

Here's the concept. Now that we have joined the Common Market it is particularly deplorable, in my opinion, that magazines of the sort that male readers participate in privately with the door shut still consider exotic locations abroad as the proper setting for figure shooting on the sands.

What's wrong with this country? Why does it always have to be Denise, Stephanie, Fifi and Kerry-Jane soaking up the sun on the beaches of Ibiza and then joining the photographer, Heinz, in the champagne a go-go bar of the Hotel Player Real?

Why not Denise, Stephanie, Fifi and Kerry-Jane in the car-park of the Red Bull Hotel Staines and, later, enjoying a shandy with the photographer, Henry de Root, in the Executives Bar of the same hotel?

I invisage a lay-out for 'Penthouse' entitled 'Away Day in Staines' and to this end I would like to book four of your best types while the weather holds.

Please let me know what would be the price of each girl for participating in erotic tableaux in Staines throughout the day and early evening (nothing distasteful).

I look forward to hearing from you.

Yours sincerely,

Henry de Root. Photographer.

Petal Model Agency,
28 Walpole Street,
London, S.W.3.   16th June 1979.

Dear Sir or Madame,

Why haven't I heard from you in reply to my letter of
6th June with regard to the proposed lay-out in
'Penthouse'?

Never mind! I can come to you! I'll hop into your
office at 3.30 pm on Tuesday 26th June to run my eye up
and down a line-up of your best types.

Do you happen to represent the delightful lass
currently participating in the 'Lilt' commercial on TV
(television)? If you do, get her there on the 26th. She'd
be fine for what I have in mind. Also those two blonde
girls – don't know their names, I'm afraid – who apart
from modelling without benefit of clothes also form a
popular singing duo. I think one of them may be called
Nina. Or if it's not her, then it's the other one. Have
them there on Tuesday week if you represent them.
Plus any others you deem appropriate to my concept.

I look forward to becoming acquainted with you and
the girls on the 26th. Kindly let me know well in
advance if for any reason this date is not suitable for

you. I'd hate to run through your door and find no one there but a couple of dozey typists painting their finger-nails and considering their personal involvements.

Let's make money here!

Yours sincerely,

Henry de Root.

PETAL

Petal Model Agency Ltd. 28 Walpole Street, Chelsea, London, SW3 4QS.

Mr. Henry de Root,
138 Elm Park Mansions,
Park Walk, London, S.W.10.   18th June, 1979

Dear Mr. de Root,

Thank you for your letter of the 16th June.

Unfortunately we do not have any models suitable for your proposed lay-out for 'Penthouse'.

The model in the 'Lilt' advertisement is Stefanie Marrian, who is with Askew's model agency. Also the two blond models you mentioned are currently making a record but can be found at Bobton's.

I'm sorry we can't help you, but perhaps you could ring Geoff Wootton Agency 736 0191.

Yours sincerely,

Dawn Wylie-Harris.

139 Elm Park Mansions
Park Walk
London, S.W.10.

The Director of Public Prosecutions,
The DPP's Office,
4 Queen Anne's Gate,
London, S.W.1.   19th June 1979.

Sir,

I have before me the so-called girlie magazine
Penthouse, Vol 14 No 4, and refer specifically to 'Emma
Jane's Diary' which purports to be a regular column
written by a self-alleged call-girl entitled Miss Emma
Jane Crampton.

I make no comment on the fact that a call-girl is
allowed to advertise her services by writing a column in
a widely read magazine. That the authorities allow such
a state of affairs to continue hardly surprises one these
days.

However, I do object most strongly to her opening
remarks, which read as follows:

'Disgusted to find in my 'Observer' today a long and
sycophantic interview with the increasingly absurd Mrs
Thatcher, in the course of which she keeps referring to
something she calls 'ordinary folk'. It so happens that I
shall shortly be interviewing Mrs Thatcher myself on
behalf of 'Penthouse' and I can say here and now that if
she dares to call me 'an ordinary folk' I shall lean
forward and, with one deft movement, pull her
knickers down.'

Can one say this? Surely any unauthorised reference

to Mrs Thatcher's knickers is illegal and a threat to pull them down by a private citizen unaquainted with Mrs Thatcher tantamount to civil disorder? So-called Miss Crampton continues:

'In my experience most suburban ladies find it a most disconcerting tactic and I urge 'ordinary folk' throughout the land to adopt this highly effective form of political comment should they have the misfortune to meet Mrs Thatcher in the course of one of her vote-losing walk-abouts'.

There we have it! A direct instruction to ordinary folk everywhere (and what's wrong with being an ordinary folk, I might ask?) to pull our Leader's knickers down! And what could be more offensive than Miss Crampton's suggestion that only suburban ladies would find such treatment discouraging? She continues:

'I assure you that the manoeuvre is easier than you might suppose – the element of surprise usually proving decisive. I did it to Mrs Whitehouse outside the Old Bailey after the Gay News trial and, as you will have seen for yourselves, she hasn't been the same since'.

I look forward to receiving your assurance, Sir, that you have already started proceedings against Miss Emma Jane Crampton and the magazine for which she writes. Failing this, I must tell you that I shall have no hesitation in instigating a private prosecution.

I am not without means and am aquainted with Sir James Goldsmith.

Yours faithfully,

Henry Root.

Copy to Mrs Mary Whitehouse.

National Viewers and Listeners' Association

Mr. Henry Root,
139 Elm Park Mansions,
Park Walk,
London SW10.   26th June 1979.

Dear Mr. Root,

Thank you very much for your letter of 19th June and for the copy of the letter you have sent to the Director of Public Prosecutions.

Miss Crampton's story is pure fabrication as far as I am concerned – I am grateful for your concern over this but I am of the opinion that any legal action on our part over this would simply give publicity to this very stupid woman.

Yours sincerely,

Mary Whitehouse.

139 Elm Park Mansions
Park Walk
London, S.W.10.

The Director of Public Prosecutions,
The DPP's Office,
4 Queen Anne's Gate,
London, S.W.1.   7th August 1979.

Dear Sir,

I wrote to you on 19th June 1979 in the matter of
so-called Miss Emma Jane Crampton's suggestion in
the 'girlie' magazine 'Penthouse' that ordinary folk
should, if presented with the opportunity, pull Mrs
Thatcher's knickers down (surely there's a 'D' Notice on
these?)

I said that unless I had your immediate assurance that
you were about to institute proceedings against Miss
Crampton and the magazine for which she writes, I
would commence a private prosecution myself.

On 27th June I receive a curt printed
acknowledgement (on a postcard!), but since then I
have heard nothing.

I must ask you again, Sir, whether you intend to
prosecute 'Penthouse' and Miss Crampton, and if not,
why not.

Yours faithfully,

Henry Root.

Director of Public Prosecutions

4–12 Queen Anne's Gate London SW1H 9AZ

Mr. Harry Root
139 Elm Park Mansions
Park Walk
London
SW10.   Date   8 August 1979

Dear Sir

Thank you for your letter dated 7 August, 1979.

I do not intend to prosecute 'Penthouse' or Miss Crampton, because in my view such a course is not justified.

Yours faithfully

D. G. WILLIAMS

Assistant Director of Public Prosecutions

139 Elm Park Mansions
Park Walk
London, S.W.10.

Sir James Goldsmith,
Cavenham Foods,
Millington Road,
Hayes.

18th June 1979.

Dear Sir James,

I've been watching you for some time and you're all right! If you decide to go into politics you can count on at least one vote. Mine!

The way you stand up against the pinko conspirators in the media is an inspiration to decent folk anywhere!

If we stick together we can beat them. How much money do they have? Not enough!

Here's a pound. Although you always win your court cases against the weasels of 'Private Eye' it's my experience that cowardly bullies don't settle their bills as quickly as they promulgate an innuendo. The pound's to help you bridge the gap.

I believe you're presently showing a high profile in the publishing game. Well done! I'm about to go into publishing myself with the purchase of the house of Cape. Do you know them? All right once, not too sweet now. Perhaps we might get together on this one. I'm looking for investors so if you're interested why don't we grab a bite to eat some time?

What do you say we meet for lunch at your favourite watering-hole, the Clermont Club, on Friday 29th June?

I'd make it sooner, but I'm flat to the boards at the moment with one thing and another.

I'm not a member of the Clermont myself, but no doubt you can fix that. You get me in and I'll pay for lunch. How's that? Fair enough?

I look forward to meeting you on the 29th.

Freedom of speech except for blackmailers! Let's go!

Yours sincerely,

Henry Root.

139 Elm Park Mansions
Park Walk
London, S.W.10.

Mr A. R. Beevor,
Hambros Bank Ltd,
41 Bishopsgate,
London, E.C.2.   14th June 1979.

Dear Beevor,

   Please forgive me for not having been back to you
sooner with reference to my take-over of Jonathan Cape
Ltd.

   The fact is I've been flat to the boards here trying to
raise the wind to get the caper off the ground.

   Don't hesitate to let me know if you have any sharp
ideas yourself in this direction! I could use them!

   Stay cool. I'll be back to you soon.

Yours sincerely,

Henry Root.

65–68 Leadenhall Street
London,
EC3A 2BA.

Henry Root, Esq.,
139 Elm Park Mansions,
Park Walk,
London SW10   20th June 1979

Dear Mr. Root,

Thank you very much for your letter which I
appreciated enormously. I am grateful for the £1 which I
will send to the appropriate charity for retired
journalists. I do so because I know that the bulk of them
are decent.

I wish you much good luck in your new venture. At
the moment I am fully involved in my own publishing
venture and I am afraid NOW magazine will take up all
the time and financial resources currently available!

Perhaps a little later in the year we can be in touch
again.

Yours sincerely,

James Goldsmith

139 Elm Park Mansions
Park Walk
London, S.W.10.

Mr Paul Johnson,
The Evening Standard,
Fleet Street,
London, E.C.4.   30th May 1979.

Dear Johnson,

I would like you to know how much I appreciate your
articles in various newspapers and periodicals. More
than any other journalist, you did more, it seems to me,
to ensure that in the recent election only a very small
majority voted against Mrs Thatcher.

I write to you now, in fact, concerning your article in
yesterday's 'Evening Standard', entitled 'Will Norman
stop the Tate dropping bricks?'

'Of all Margaret Thatcher's appointments,' you
wrote, 'the one which I have heard most widely
applauded – at any rate among the London
intelligensia – is her decision to give Norman St John
Stevas responsibility for the arts'.

I don't doubt you're right, but can you tell me who
precisely constitutes 'the London intelligensia' and
where they live? It seems to me that they must be an
exceptionally close-knit group, all living in the same
vicinity and meeting every evening, otherwise even
someone as well-connected as you could not, in the
relatively short time since the election, have canvassed
their opinion of Norman's appointment.

As a plain man who's kicked up it's never been my
privilege to meet 'London's intelligensia' and I'd like to

[212]

put this right before it's too late. Can you advise me how to set about it?

A little later in the same article you say 'Norman is an experienced boulevardier'. What's this exactly? I don't speak much French, but a literal translation would seem to suggest that Norman's an experienced street-walker. Can this really be the case? Does Mrs Thatcher know?

I'd be most grateful if you could clear up these two problems for me. I wouldn't normally trouble such a busy and important person with trivialities of this nature, but it's always struck me that, though an aristocrat yourself, you care about the problems of those you refer to as 'the people'.

Yours sincerely,

Henry Root.

Copy to The Rt Hon Norman St John Stevas.

Saturday, 7th July 1979

Please accept my apologies for not having answered your letter before. I have been in Washington, then in the Middle East, and have many unanswered letters. I have no secretary at present and large numbers of people write to me, often posing questions I cannot answer. A boulevardier is a man-about-town who knows his way around; but how you are to meet the intelligensia is a query which cannot be satisfied if it is necessary to frame it.

Paul Johnson.

139 Elm Park Mansions
Park Walk
London, S.W.10.

The Officer-in-Charge,
The Criminal Record Office,
New Scotland Yard,
London, S.W.1.   30th May 1979.

Sir,

  I would be grateful if you would run the following
people through the computor at Hendon and let me
know whether they all come up brand new. I don't
think my reasons for wanting this information need
concern you. Suffice it to say that they are people with
whom I may be coming into contact, socially or in a
business context, in the near future.

  Mr Ray Cooney. Impresario and immigrant (possibly
illegal). c/o The Whitehall Theatre, London,

  Mr Edward du Cann, MP and one-time chairman of
Keyser Ullman Ltd of Milk Street, E.C.1. (not an
address to inspire confidence). Rumoured to be
descended from Miss Nell Gwynne.

  Mr Russell Harty Plos. Chat show host. London
Weekend Television Ltd, London, S.E.1.

  Mr Norman St John Stevas. Minister for 'the Arts'.
Alleged to be a boulevardier (or streetwalker.)

  Mr Jonathan Cape (deceased). Publisher. Late of 30
Bedford Square, London, W.C.1.

  Mr Richard West. Cricket commentator, Rugby

correspondent of 'The Times', one time 'host' of 'Come Dancing' and presently Morals Correspondent of 'The Spectator', 56 Doughty Street, London, W.C.1.

Thanking you.

Yours faithfully,

Henry Root.

139 Elm Park Mansions
Park Walk
London, S.W.10.

The Officer in Charge
Criminal Records Office,
New Scotland Yard,
London, S.W.1.   16th June 1979

Dear Sir,

Did you get my letter of 30th May asking you to feed
certain people through your compuptor at Hendon?

I imagine you can't have done, otherwise I would
have heard from you by now.

If it always took as long as this to check out someone's
deep background and personal standards you'd never
catch anyone, least of all other policemen!

They'd be up and away while you were waiting for
the print-out!

Let me know if you didn't get my letter and I'll send
you a copy.

Yours faithfully,

Henry Root.

139 Elm Park Mansions
Park Walk
London, S.W.10.

The Officer-in-Charge,
Criminal Records Office,
New Scotland Yard,
London, S.W.1.   3rd July 1979.

Dear Sir,

I've been sitting here wondering why you haven't replied to my letters of 30th May and 16th June, requesting you to feed certain 'faces' through your computor.

Now I know! I should have bunged you!

Reporting the case of The Police and The Playboy Club v Ladbrooks Ltd in the matter of the Gaming Act, today's 'Daily Express' tells us that for a private citizen to obtain confidential information from the computor a 'drop' of 50p per name is levied by the policeman in charge.

Sorry! I should have been cognisant of this.

Although there were six names on my list originally, my own 'people' have been able to discover all anyone would want to know about Mr Richard West and Mr Russell Harty Plos. I now only need the deep background on Mr Ray Cooney, Mr Edward Du Cann, Mr Norman St John Stevas and Mr Jonathan Cape.

I enclose £2 being 50p for each name.

Sorry about my ignorance of the 'system'.

Yours faithfully,

Henry Root.

139 Elm Park Mansions
Park Walk
London, S.W.10.

The Commanding Officer,
'B' Division (the best!),
Chelsea Police Station,
2 Lucan Place,
London, S.W.3.   21st July 1979.

Dear Commander,

Over the past few weeks I have been corresponding
with the Criminal Records Office at Scotland Yard re
getting the deep background on certain people with
whom I was about to come in contact.

Receiving no reply to my letters, I eventually sent
them a couple of pounds to 'aid the due processes', as
it were.

On the morning of Friday 13th July, two of your best
men (an Inspector and a Sergeant) ran through my door
with two pounds in an envelope and pointed out that
'dropping' the CRO wasn't good form.

Fair enough. However, they also pointed out that I
had wasted their valuable time. Being a great supporter
of Law and Order (particularly in Chelsea) I feel rather
bad about this. In the circumstances I would like to
make a contribution to a police charity which is on the
up-and-up and I consequently now return the two
pounds. I recently sent a fiver to Sir David McNee and
he popped it into the Police Dependants' Trust. That
would be fine by me.

The post being what it is these days (don't worry –

Sir Keith Joseph will get that right), I'd like to hear that the money has arrived safely, but please don't bother to send any of your young men round to thank me personally.

Yours sincerely,

Henry Root.

139 Elm Park Mansions
Park Walk
London, S.W.10.

Sir Joseph Cantley,
Carpmael Buildings,
Temple,
London, E.C.4.   6th July 1979.

M'Lud,

Now that the dust's settled after the so-called 'Trial of
the Century', I judge it to be the time to congratulate
you on the fine showing you put up throughout. You
tipped the jury the right way and some of your jokes
were first-class! Well done!

Some folk thought Thorpe was for the high jump at
last, but you never looked to me like the sort of man
who'd send an Old Etonian to the pokey on the say-so
of an Italian air-line pilot, a discredited businessman
with dyed hair from L.A. (Los Angeles) a dusky-hued
character from the Channel Islands and a 'male model'
with the unlikely name of Josiffe.

What a courageous example Mrs Thorpe set by the
way she 'stood by' her husband throughout his ordeal!
(Perhaps you could have made more of this in your
closing speech for the defence). Most wives would have
popped the family valuables and had it away on their
toes to South America. And where, might I ask, were
the wives of Bessell, Josiffe and 'Gino' Newton?
Conspicuous by their absence!

Here's a pound. I would have sent it to you during
the trial, but I was advised that you might rule this
contempt of court and pack me off with my tooth-brush

for a night or two in Brixton! It might also have been construed as an attempt to pervert the course of justice, and I knew I could safely leave that to you.

Yours respectfully,

Henry Root.

139 Elm Park Mansions
Park Walk
London, S.W.10.

The Commissioner,
The City of London Police,
26 Old Jewry,
London, E.C.2.   24th July 1979.

Dear Commissioner,

Some two weeks ago I had occasion to send a pound
to Mr Justice Cantley. This was a token of my esteem
following the way he conducted himself during the
so-called Thorpe trial.

Imagine my surprise, last Friday morning, when two
of your officers returned this money in person on the
grounds that His Lordship didn't need it at the
moment. They were most courteous, of course, but did
murmur something about it being a waste of time and
money having to hop round to my place personally.
Being a great supporter of the force (and a friend of Mr
James Anderton, the Chief Constable of Manchester) I
was somewhat shocked to think that I of all people had
been responsible for using up the time of two fine
young officers who would have been better employed
clearing our streets of punks, muggers and
demonstrating mimes on their way to pester Mrs
Thatcher re VAT.

In the circumstances, I am now returning the pound
(it may not be the same one, I'm afraid – money slips
through the fingers so quickly these days, don't you
find?) and I would be most pleased if you'd put it
towards some worthy police charity.

[224]

I'd like to know that this small contribution to the fight against orchestrated extremism has arrived safely (the post being what it is these days – no marks to Sir William Barlowe!), but please don't bother to send any of your men round to thank me personally. Frankly the sudden presence in my lounge-room of two young constables on duty can have a negative bearing on a business deal. I'm sure you'll understand.

Yours sincerely,

Henry Root.

City of London Police

26 Old Jewry,
London, EC2R 8DJ

6th August, 1979

Dear Mr Root,

I am directed by the Commissioner of Police for the City of London to thank you for your letter of 24th July, 1979 and acknowledge safe receipt of your kind donation of £1.00, which has been allocated to the City of London Police Benevolent Fund as you requested.

Yours sincerely,

A/Chief Superintendent

H Root Esq
139 Elm Park Mansions
Park Walk
London SW10

139 Elm Park Mansions
Park Walk
London, S.W.10.

Mr Kenneth Kendall,
BBC News,
Lime Grove,
London, W.12.   12th July 1979.

Dear Kenneth,

I hope you won't mind my calling you Kenneth. Your
face has been appearing for so long in my lounge-room
that I feel you're a friend of the family. Still, I expect
that's what they all say.

Sorry to read in the paper today that your teeth fell
out while you were reading the news last night. Most
awkward for you.

Here's a pound. Get yourself a tube of Dentu-Fix, but
be careful where you keep it. Mrs Snipe, who lives
opposite, confused hers with the Polyfilla tube and all
her windows fell out.

How about a photo for Mrs Root? You're her
favourite newscaster. Do you merely read the news or
do you make it up as well? I've often wondered.

All the best,

Yours sincerely,

Henry Root.

British Broadcasting Corporation

Television Centre Wood Lane London W12 7RJ

July 23rd 1979

Dear Henry,

Thank you for the sympathetic note and the £1! All charges for fixing the fallen crown will be borne by my dentist and if Dentu-fix is needed he can jolly well supply it – so here's your £1 back!

No, we don't write the news – we read it.

I enclose a photo for Mrs Root.

All good wishes

Kenneth Kendall

139 Elm Park Mansions
Park Walk
London, S.W.10.

Lord Ted Dexter,
The Sunday Mirror,
Holborn Circus,
London, E.C.1.

18th July 1979.

My Lord!

Your articles in 'The Sunday Mirror' are often good, as are your live commentaries on TV. Well done! It seemed to me that after lunch in the last Test you had difficulty getting your tongue round the names of our Indian friends. Here's a tip. Don't bother with their names. Just say: "Oh dear! The ball went straight through the little sooty's legs!" That sort of thing.

I write to you now to ask your opinion of our present skipper, Brearley. He is more to blame than anyone, it seems to me, for the introduction of compulsory crash helmets when batting. I appreciate that he's an intellectual and as such will not wish to have his brains rattled too often by a piece of hard leather travelling at speed, but how many of those under him are intellectuals? None at all, I'd guess, least of all the lad Botham and the big man, Hendrick. 'Rags' too strikes me as being alert in the field rather than a deep thinker. So what's their excuse? I myself have been hit on the head many times and this didn't stop me getting to the top in fish.

I was concerned too by certain passages in Brearley's book now being serialised in 'The Observer'. On the recent tour of Australia horse-play took place, it seems, with the skipper's approval, with the lad Botham putting himself about the English dressing-room and introducing ice-cubes into Boycott's socks. Did this sort of thing go on in your day? Surely not!

I'm not happy either about all the pansy kissing and hand-holding which now takes place in the middle, particularly at the fall of a wicket. The photo above Brearley's article in yesterday's 'Observer' of Botham clasping the boy Gower to his bosom might well have been misconstrued by those of a mind to do so.

What's your opinion of these developments?

Could you oblige with a photo? I'd like to stick it up in my boy Henry Jr's room as an example of what can be done with an upright stance and a straight bat. You were a true Corinthian and some of your drives through mid-off would, on contact, have loosened a rhino's balls. Of how many can one say that these days?

Yours ever,

Henry Root.

Monday

Dear Mr Root,

I don't keep pics about the place these days – sorry.

Hope your lad goes the right way with his cricket.

Keep him *sideways* both batting and bowling.

I never see people make many runs with helmets!

Sincerely,

Tex Dexter

Mr Peter Saunders,
The Mousetrap Man!,
The Vaudeville Theatre,
London, W.C.2.   23rd July 1979.

Dear Mr Saunders,

May I be the first to congratulate you on your
engagement to the TV personality, Lady Katie Boyle?
She's still a handsome woman and her advice at the
back of 'The TV Times' is sometimes sound.

That's enough of that – down to business! As far as I
know you've never put on a dirty show (well done!) so I
am now enclosing for your evaluation my original stage
play THE ENGLISH WAY OF DOING THINGS by
HENRY ROOT. You'll find it an amusing romp in two
acts with only enough unnecessary explicitness to suck
in our Japanese friends over here to photograph Her
Majesty and buy their underwear in Oxford Street.

I'd be prepared to take your theatre for a season on
sensible terms. I read in 'The Sunday Express' the other
day that you keep in your office a fridge full of
champagne for visiting actors and other more serious
folk, so unless I hear from you to the contrary I'll drop in
on you at about 11.30 on Tuesday 7th August to discuss
the deal. This will give you more than a week to assess
the play's potential and jot down casting ideas (though
I'll have the final say, of course, in this department.)

Have you come across the work of an actress called
Glenda Jackson? She'd be fine for the part of the old

boiler who comes to grief early in Act 1, but don't waste your time considering 'Sir' Robert Mark for the role of the stupid Police Commissioner because he's already turned it down on the grounds that he doesn't after all want to be an actor (after his TV deodorant commercial who's surprised?)

I'd want first crack at the ingenue, of course, but you could be second cab off the rank. I'd not say a word to your good lady as long as you didn't drop me in it with Mrs Root!

Who gets the ice-cream sales? Do we share? I'll take care of the critics. A fiver's on its way to Irving Warble of 'The Times' and since Mrs Root is about to join Arriana Stassinopulos's 'Levitation and Deep Personal Awareness' group I'll be able to 'get to' Bernard Levin.

Let's make money here!

Yours for family theatre,

Henry Root.

Enc: THE ENGLISH WAY OF DOING THINGS by HENRY ROOT.

Peter Saunders Ltd

Vaudeville Theatre Offices
10, Maiden Lane, London WC2E 7NA

Henry Root Esq
139 Elm Park Mansions
Park Walk
LONDON SW10

30th July 1979

Dear Mr Root

Thank you for your letter of the 25th July and for your congratulations.

Please don't come in on the 7th August as firstly, as I have a meeting which will last most of the day and secondly, I have quite a stock of plays to read and it is better to see if I like it first.

Yours sincerely

PETER SAUNDERS

Peter Saunders Ltd

Vaudeville Theatre Offices
10, Maiden Lane, London, WC2E 7NA

Henry Root Esq
139 Elm Park Mansions
Park Walk
LONDON SW10   5th September 1979

Dear Mr Root

   "The English Way of Doing Things" by *Henry Root*

   Thank you for sending me this play but I don't think it
is one that I would care to take on especially as I have
another attraction to follow the current one at the
Vaudeville.

   Of course, I do indeed know Glenda Jackson but she
has committed herself to another play in February of
next year.

   I am so sorry not to be more helpful but I don't think a
meeting would really serve any purpose.

Yours sincerely

PETER SAUNDERS

Enc

139 Elm Park Mansions
Park Walk
London, S.W.10.

Ms Debra Byron,
Jonathan Cape Ltd,
30 Bedford Square,
London, W.C.1.

29th August 1979.

Dear Ms Byron,

You'll be wondering why you haven't heard from me since your sensible letter of 6th June.

Don't worry! I've been hard at work on a money-making concept that could do us both a bit of good.

Have you by any chance heard of a book entitled 'Man Watching' by a keeper at the London Zoo called Desmond Morris? I imagine you may have done because your outfit published it. It's a psychological pot-boiler, lacking that certain something to take it to the top of the hot-hundred list, but at least it had the merit of giving me this solid idea.

How about WOMAN WATCHING by HENRY ROOT? Who do you think? And it would have the added advantage of being comprehensively illustrated by myself. You may not be aware that as well as being a wirter I am also a fully equipped photographer of style ever at the ready with my system set, so I am taking this opportunity of enclosing my portfolio of girls snapped from an unexpected angle.

Here's the scheme. Financed by you I'll lurk unusually in places not normally available to men. No doubt you will yourself have visited 'The Sanctuary' in Covent Garden, a 'girls only' sauna and swimming club where dancers and others of that ilk strip off and recline on benches. With a letter of introduction from you, I'll hop incognito through the door in a pair of ballet pumps and, with a cry of "Straighten up ladies! I've been sent by Cape!", I'll take unusual photos before ejection.

How does it strike you? Let's be positive on this one!

What I need is a letter of authority from you enabling me to enter premises not generally available for figure shooting in the afternoon. I suggest something along the following lines:

TO WHOM IT MAY CONCERN:

This is to confirm that Mr Henry Root is engaged for us on a viable undertaking entitled WOMAN WATCHING. We would be most grateful if you could give him your full cooperation and, after he has finished, forward the account to us for settlement.

Signed: Debra Byron.
p.p. Jonathan Cape Ltd.

With your help I should be able to have the first draft on your desk by the end of October.

Let's go!

Yours sincerely,

Henry Root.

P.S. In case you're of a mind to utilise my photos to

illustrate other books in your pipe-line, I should warn you that they are fully protected by the Copyright Act 1959, and I enclose a stamped addressed envelope for their safe return.

Jonathan Cape Limited

Thirty Bedford Square
London W.C.1.

Mr Henry Root,
139 Elm Park Mansions,
Park Walk,
London, S.W.10.   31st August, 1979.

Dear Mr Root,

Thank you for your letter of 29th August together with
photographs. We regret that we do not think it would
be worth your while sending us a finished copy of
WOMAN WATCHING. We wish you success in
placing it elsewhere.

Please find your photographs enclosed.

Yours sincerely,

Debra Byron,
Editorial.

139 Elm Park Mansions
Park Walk
London, S.W.10.

The Headmaster,
Langley Grammar School,
Langley,
Berks.   27th July 1979.

Dear Headmaster,

My friend Paul Johnson – who, as you may or may
not know, is one of Mrs Thatcher's closest advisers –
recently wrote in 'The Evening Standard' that your
school isn't a seminary for subversives, has no great
reputation for Marxist studies, drugs or violence and
that its staff do not spend their spare time engaged in
race-demos and assaults on the police.

Well done!

In the circumstances I'm prepared to entrust to your
care my boy Henry Jr, now 15. Frankly, he's not
shaping up. He wears girls' blouses and plays the guitar
to excess. We all know where that leads. A recent study
shows that *one hundred per cent* of youngsters on hard
drugs had at some time in their lives listened to so-
called pop music.

When can he start? On the assumption that you
believe in private enterprise, I enclose a fiver. This is for
you personally, you understand, and is merely the tip
of the ice-berg. There's more to come if you manage to
slip him to the top of the queue.

I'll pay generously for what I want, so if there's anything you need – a new pav for the playing fields,

perhaps, or a colour TV for the Senior Common Room –
just let me know.

Shall I come and see you? Just give me the word and I
can be your way in 24 hours.

I look forward to doing business with you.

How are you off for fish?

Support Mrs Thatcher!

Yours sincerely,

Henry Root.

P.S. I take it capital punishment still takes place in your
school. Let me know about this. Youngsters must learn
what's what.

Langley Grammar School

Headmaster:
A. G. Robinson, M.Sc. Ph.D., C Chem., F.R.I.C.

16 August 1979

Henry Root Esq
139 Elm Park Mansions
Park Walk
London SW 10

Dear Mr Root

Thank you for your letter of the 27 July enquiring about a possible place here for Henry Junior.

The only possible suggestion which I can make is that we test Henry here at the school with a view to him entering our 5th year. The criterion for entry is usually the 12+ selection test conducted by the Berkshire County Council. The staff would be prepared to test him at this stage in the various subjects. If he was successful a place would be offered. You would then have to write to the Director of Education at Kennet House, King's Road, Reading, with a view to having this confirmed. The difficulty would be the fact that you reside in Greater London and this means taking the matter up with them as well.

We assemble back for the Autumn Term on Tuesday, September 4th and if you wished us to proceed with the testing this will be arranged. Perhaps you would kindly let me know if you wish this to take place.

I am on holiday 17 – 31 August so if you contacted me on the phone here at the school, Slough 43222, on Tuesday 4 September I will then be in a position to suggest a date for testing.

Many thanks for your kind comments about the school. I am forwarding your £5 to the treasurer of the Langley Grammar School Fighting Fund and he will send you a receipt in due course.

Looking forward to seeing you.

Yours sincerely

Headmaster

Dictated by Dr Robinson but signed in his absence.

139 Elm Park Mansions
Park Walk
London, S.W.10.

The Senior Tutor,
Magdalene College,
Cambridge.

29th July 1979.

Dear Senior Tutor,

Yours is a college at which brains are neither here nor there, I'm told. Indeed, my enquiries lead me to understand that duffers are more than welcome so long as their fathers measure up financially.

This being the case, I'm prepared to send my boy to you in three years time. He's 15 now and shows every sign of needing all the advantages money can buy. You'll have seen many like that.

I'll leave the subject to you. *Not* sociology.

Places are tight, I dare say, (many being snapped up at birth by Etonians and such) but I'm prepared to pay 'over the top' to achieve equality of opportunity. That's the Tory way. We voted for Mrs Thatcher so that those of us who had indulged in prudent house-keeping down the years could give their youngsters a flying start.

I enclose a small cash advance (this is for you personally, you understand) against a heavy financial contribution to the college if you can 'fix' a place for my boy.

What do you need? Do you have a decent library? If not, just say the word. I'd be happy to endow you with sufficient funds to build one. I'd want some sort of credit, of course. Something along the lines of 'This Library has been generously gifted to the College by Henry Root Wet Fish Ltd'. If you wanted to put this in Latin, that would be okay with me. Or what about a new pavillion for your playing-field? What, come to that, about a new playing-field? Exercise, in my experience, takes boys' minds off matters on which they'd be better not to dwell till later.

I look forward to hearing from you.

Yours against student participation,

Henry Root.

T. E. B. HOWARD, M.C., M.A.
Senior Tutor and Tutor for Admissions

Magdalene College

Cambridge, CB3 0AG

Henry Root Esq.,
139 Elm Park Mansions,
Park Walk,
London, S.W.10.   31 July 1979

Dear Mr. Root,

Thank you for your letter. I am afraid I do not know
who you are, but you are evidently either an ingenious
hoaxer or labouring under a massive misapprehension.
I therefore return your £5 note herewith.

Yours sincerely,

Major-General Wyldbore-Smith, C.B., D.S.O., O.B.E.,
Conservative Board of Finance,
32 Smith Square,
Westminster,
London, S.W.1.   7th August 1979.

Dear Major-General Wyldbore-Smith,

I'm a blunt man, accustomed to plain-speaking, so I'll
come straight to the point.

What's the going price for getting an honour?

I'm not talking about an M.B.E., an O.B.E. or a C.B.E.
They seem to be for ballet dancers, disc-jockeys,
crooners and those who are quick over the high
hurdles. (No offence meant. I see that you yourself have
the O.B.E. Nothing wrong with that. Well done!) No,
I'm talking about a life peerage, or, at the very least, a
knighthood like my friend Sir James Goldsmith.

In the course of the past year I have contributed
steadily and generously to Tory Party funds. Your
understrapper Brigadier L. H. Lee C.B.E. will confirm
this. (I am writing to you rather than him, incidentally,
because you seem to outrank him and because you have
the more sensible name.) I realise, however, that I will
have to think in terms of a rather more substantial lump
sum in order to secure a place near the top of Mrs
Thatcher's New Year hand-outs.

Can you give me an idea of the approximate amount?

[247]

I read recently that a 'drop' of as little as £25,000 to one of our leading politicians was enough to obtain a seat in the Lords for the donor.

Has inflation bumped up the price?

Let me know. I'm waiting here with my cheque-book ready!

Support Mrs Thatcher!

Yours sincerely,

Henry Root.

P.S. It goes without saying that there could be 'something in this' for you personally.

Conservative Board of Finance

32 Smith Square,
Westminster, SW1P 3HH

14th August 1979

Henry Root Esq.,
139 Elm Park Mansions
Park Walk
London SW10

Dear Mr. Root,

Thank you for your letter of the 7th August. I think I must make it absolutely clear that there is no question of buying Honours from the Conservative Party.

However, I am most grateful to you for the support which you have given to the Party over the past few months.

Yours sincerely,

F. B. Wyldbore-Smith

139 Elm Park Mansions
Park Walk
London, S.W.10.

Mr Simon Dally,
Weidenfeld & Nicolson Ltd,
91 Clapham High Street,
London, S.W.4.   16th June 1979

Dear Mr Dally,

Many thanks for your kind letter of 13th June.

I appreciate your offer and encouraging remarks
about my book, but I'm afraid I have to tell you that I
have thought it best to put the whole matter into the
hands of an experienced literary agent.

I am now exclusively represented by Miss Hilary
Rubinstein of A. P. Watt & Son (perhaps you know her)
and I must ask you to *do nothing* until you hear from
her.

Yours sincerely,

Henry Root.

139 Elm Park Mansions
Park Walk
London, S.W.10.

Mr Simon Dally,
Weidenfeld & Nicolson Ltd,
91 Clapham High Street,
London, S.W.4.   22nd June 1979.

Dear Mr Dally,

Good news! I've dumped Miss Rubinstein! She left me no alternative. I couldn't have my literary agent blackguarding my publisher like that. The things she said about your offer!

The long and short of it is that I told her to get on her bike and that I could handle myself. "I never doubted it," she said. I don't know what she meant by that.

So – the book's yours! After due consideration I have decided that I'd rather hand over a gallon of petrol than all that cash (£200,000! That's more than I make in a whole year!), so if you make representation to the Park Walk Garage (352 9727) and ask for the General he'll confirm that there's a can there (4 star!) in the name of Lord Weidenfeld. I know you told me that under your new accounting system all cheques and emoluments are made out to you (well done!) but I judged it best to row in Lord W. at an early stage. I don't want to get off on the wrong foot with the man at the top. I'm sure you'll understand.

Incidentally, for the last few months I haven't just been sitting here trying to get my novel off the ground. I have made it my business to correspond with folk of consequence in all walks of life on appertaining issues. I have in my possession telling letters from such public persons as Mrs Thatcher, Mr Brian Clough, His Excellency the South African Ambassador, Miss Esther Rantzen, the Lord Chancellor, the First Sea Lord and Miss Angela Rippon.

Would you like to see them? They make a valid contribution, in my opinion, to the great debate.

I look forward to hearing from you.

Yours sincerely,

Henry Root.

All Futura Books are available at your bookshop or
newsagent, or can be ordered from the following
address:
Futura Books, Cash Sales Department,
P.O. Box 11, Falmouth, Cornwall.

Please send cheque or postal order (no currency), and
allow 30p for postage and packing for the first book
plus 15p for the second book and 12p for each additional
book ordered up to a maximum charge of £1.29 in U.K.

Customers in Eire and B.F.P.O. please allow 30p for
the first book, 15p for the second book plus 12p per
copy for the next 7 books, thereafter 6p per book.

Overseas customers please allow 50p for postage and
packing for the first book and 10p per copy for each
additional book.